PETER HO-SUN CHAN'S
He's a Woman,
She's a Man

Hong Kong University Press thanks Xu Bing for writing the Press's name in his Square Word Calligraphy for the covers of its books. For further information see p. iv.

THE NEW HONG KONG CINEMA SERIES

The New Hong Kong Cinema came into existence under very special circumstances, during a period of social and political crisis resulting in a change of cultural paradigms. Such critical moments have produced the cinematic achievements of the early Soviet cinema, neorealism, the *nouvelle vague*, and the German cinema of the 1970s and, we can now say, the New Hong Kong Cinema. If this cinema grew increasingly intriguing in the 1980s, after the announcement of Hong Kong's return to China, it is largely because it had to confront a new cultural and political space that was both complex and hard to define, where the problems of colonialism were uncannily overlaid with those of globalism. Such uncanniness could not be caught through straight documentary or conventional history writing: it was left to the cinema to define it.

Has the creative period of the New Hong Kong Cinema now come to an end? However we answer the question, there is a need to evaluate the achievements of Hong Kong cinema. This series distinguishes itself from the other books on the subject by focusing in-depth on individual Hong Kong films, which together make the New Hong Kong Cinema.

Series General Editors
Ackbar Abbas, Wimal Dissanayake, Mette Hjort, Gina Marchetti, Stephen Teo

Series Advisors
Chris Berry, Nick Browne, Ann Hui, Leo Lee, Li Cheuk-to, Patricia Mellencamp, Meaghan Morris, Paul Willemen, Peter Wollen, Wu Hung

Other titles in the series
Andrew Lau and Alan Mak's *Infernal Affairs – The Trilogy* by Gina Marchetti
Fruit Chan's *Durian Durian* by Wendy Gan
John Woo's *A Better Tomorrow* by Karen Fang
John Woo's *Bullet in the Head* by Tony Williams
John Woo's *The Killer* by Kenneth E. Hall
Johnnie To Kei-fung's *PTU* by Michael Ingham
King Hu's *A Touch of Zen* by Stephen Teo
Mabel Cheung Yuen-ting's *An Autumn's Tale* by Stacilee Ford
Stanley Kwan's *Center Stage* by Mette Hjort
Tsui Hark's *Zu: Warriors From the Magic Mountain* by Andrew Schroeder
Wong Kar-wai's *Ashes of Time* by Wimal Dissanayake
Wong Kar-wai's *Happy Together* by Jeremy Tambling
Yuen Woo-ping's *Wing Chun* by Sasha Vojković

PETER HO-SUN CHAN'S
He's a Woman, She's a Man

Lisa Odham Stokes

香港大學出版社
HONG KONG UNIVERSITY PRESS

Hong Kong University Press
14/F Hing Wai Centre
7 Tin Wan Praya Road
Aberdeen
Hong Kong

ISBN 978-962-209-970-8

British Library Cataloguing-in-Publication Data
A catalogue record for this book is available from the British Library.

Secure on-line Ordering
http://www.hkupress.org

Printed and bound by Condor Production Ltd., Hong Kong, China

Hong Kong University Press is honoured that Xu Bing, whose art explores the complex themes of language across cultures, has written the Press's name in his Square Word Calligraphy. This signals our commitment to cross-cultural thinking and the distinctive nature of our English-language books published in China.

"At first glance, Square Word Calligraphy appears to be nothing more unusual than Chinese characters, but in fact it is a new way of rendering English words in the format of a square so they resemble Chinese characters. Chinese viewers expect to be able to read Square Word Calligraphy but cannot. Western viewers, however are surprised to find they can read it. Delight erupts when meaning is unexpectedly revealed."
— Britta Erickson, *The Art of Xu Bing*

"Dogs are our link to paradise." — Milan Kundera

For Pike, Beauty, Senshin, Mancha, Gretchen, Molly, Guido, Jim, and Princess

Peter Chan with Leslie Cheung.
Photograph courtesy of Peter Chan.

Table of Contents

Series Preface

The New Hong Kong Cinema came into existence under very special circumstances, during a period of social and political crisis resulting in a change of cultural paradigms. Such critical moments have produced the cinematic achievements of the early Soviet cinema, neorealism, the *nouvelle vague*, the German cinema in the 1970s and, we can now say, the recent Hong Kong cinema. If this cinema grew increasingly intriguing in the 1980s, after the announcement of Hong Kong's return to China, it was largely because it had to confront a new cultural and political space that was both complex and hard to define, where the problems of colonialism were overlaid with those of globalism in an uncanny way. Such uncanniness could not be caught through straight documentary or conventional history writing; it was left to the cinema to define it.

It does so by presenting to us an urban space that slips away if we try to grasp it too directly, a space that cinema coaxes into existence by whatever means at its disposal. Thus it is by eschewing a narrow idea of relevance and pursuing disreputable genres like melodrama, kung fu and the fantastic that cinema brings into view something else about the city which could otherwise be missed. One classic example is Stanley Kwan's *Rouge*, which draws on the unrealistic form of the ghost story to evoke something of the uncanniness of Hong Kong's urban space. It takes a ghost to catch a ghost.

In the New Hong Kong Cinema, then, it is neither the subject matter nor a particular set of generic conventions that is paramount. In fact, many Hong Kong films begin by following generic conventions but proceed to transform them. Such transformation of genre is also the transformation of a sense of place where all the rules have quietly and deceptively changed. It is this shifting sense of place, often expressed negatively and indirectly — but in the best work always rendered precisely in (necessarily) innovative images — that is decisive for the New Hong Kong Cinema.

Has the creative period of the New Hong Kong Cinema come to an end? However we answer the question, there is a need now to evaluate the achievements of Hong Kong cinema. During the last few years, a number of full-length books have appeared, testifying to the topicality of the subject. These books survey the field with varying degrees of success, but there is yet an almost complete lack of authoritative texts focusing in depth on individual Hong Kong films. This book series on the New Hong Kong Cinema is designed to fill this lack. Each volume will be written by a scholar/ critic who will analyse each chosen film in detail and provide a critical apparatus for further discussion including filmography and bibliography.

Our objective is to produce a set of interactional and provocative readings that would make a self-aware intervention into modern Hong Kong culture. We advocate no one theoretical position; the authors will approach their chosen films from their own distinct points of vantage and interest. The aim of the series is to generate open-ended discussions of the selected films, employing diverse analytical strategies, in order to urge the readers towards self-reflective engagements with the films in particular and the Hong Kong cultural space in general. It is our hope that this series will contribute to the sharpening of Hong Kong culture's conceptions of itself.

In keeping with our conviction that film is not a self-enclosed signification system but an important cultural practice among similar others, we wish to explore how films both reflect and inflect culture. And it is useful to keep in mind that reflection of reality and reality of reflection are equally important in the understanding of cinema.

Ackbar Abbas
Wimal Dissanayake

Acknowledgements

Filmmaking is a collaborative art, and first I would like to thank the filmmakers (the director, cast, and crew of *He's a Woman, She's a Man*) without which there would be no film and therefore no book possible, and also the many audiences that have seen and responded to the film. My deepest gratitude goes to Terence Chang and Law Kar, for their continued kindness to me and their generous assistance and deep discernments when called upon. I would also like to recognize and thank those in Hong Kong who helped me in a variety of ways with helpful information and insights and reaching larger Hong Kong audiences, specifically Jeremy Fernando, Jason Ho, June Lam, Carson Lau, Paris Lau, Doris Luey, and Denise Tang. I am very grateful to my readers, some of them with a specialty in the field and others intelligent but uninformed, including some "ordinary people" like Wing … If only we could all be those special ordinary people, as Wing is described in the theme song "Chase"! My readers served not only as proofreaders but also offered suggestions and presented questions that led to new paths of investigation. Readers include Michael Hoover, Grace Kim, Karen Longtin, Jean Lukitsh, Rei Rendon, Michael Robinson, Mike Simpson, Albert Valentin and, last but not least, Tyler Stokes. I want to thank my two translators, Debbie Quach (for print material) and Jamie Wong Hei-kwan (for translation of film dialogue). Thanks go to Peter Chan's assistants, Tairy Chan and Candy Yuen, as well as Quentin Lee, for their help. Thanks also go to Gina Marchetti for thinking of me for this series, and to the series editors and advisors for accepting my proposal; I also appreciate the patience and understanding of publisher Colin Day, associate publisher Michael Duckworth, editor Ian Lok and project editor Dawn Lau, the insights of anonymous readers, and the work of the staff at Hong Kong University Press.

I would also like to acknowledge the support of my institution, particularly my dean, Dr. Annye Refoe, and department chair, Mr. Bobbie Bell, for their encouragement and aid with research and travel, providing the opportunity for fruitful exchange with colleagues and friends that cannot be underestimated. And research librarians Vickie Arthur, Kellie Diaz, and Michael Schau for their kind assistance. For many of us in the west, Professor John Lent of Temple University has been a moving force in creating a place, both physical and virtual, for us to study Asian Cinema, and to him I will always be indebted, for his generosity as a scholar and his astute mind and ability to negotiate many borders. Last of all, I would like to recognize all of the anonymous (you know who you are!) respondents, including students in my classes at Seminole Community College, for their participation in this project; films are made to be watched, interacted with, and remembered, and these watchers provided a wealth of material for this study.

1

Comedy and More

"There's a lot to be said for making people laugh. Did you know that's all that some people have?" — Preston Sturges's *Sullivan's Travels* (1941).

"When you make a movie with a schedule like in Hong Kong, you see the idea, make it and finish it. You don't always realize what you have made, you just stumble into gold, and that's exactly what happened [with *He's a Woman, She's a Man*]." — Peter Chan.[1]

Director Peter Chan's popular, light-hearted, and delightful gender-bending "romantic comedy" *He's a Woman, She's a Man (Golden Branch, Jade Leaf)/Gam ji yuk yip/Jin zhi yu ye* (1994) satisfied Hong Kong audiences and crossed over internationally.[2] Screened at the 19th Hong Kong International Film Festival, the film was described in its program by Chan as "a traditional love story with a dash of contemporary romance"; the director also stated "the message we want to get across is that feminine men are not necessarily gay and masculine women are not necessarily lesbians." In the film, Leslie Cheung plays homophobic music producer Koo Kah-ming (Sam Koo), tired of the singing star (and girlfriend) Mui Kwai (Rose) (Carina Lau) he has promoted; both he and she fall for an "ordinary person," Lam Chi-wing (Wing) (Anita Yuen), a fan whom Sam remakes into an androgynous new singing star (actually female but whom the public and both Sam and Rose believe to be male). The plot involves events that could potentially happen in real life, but introduces coincidences and twists that are also improbable. The comedy zeroes in on Hong Kong's fascination with star celebrities, and while the story is set in the music world, the situation is as much about the film industry as it is about the music industry.[3] Gender issues, sexual orientations, identity, image-making, and the selling of images to an audience as commodities are the foci of the movie.

Comedies are not normally given their due and are easily dismissed as escapist entertainment, as American director and writer about film Peter Bogdanovich reminds us: "Comedy is always taken somewhat for granted, even though anyone who's ever done both will tell you, comedy requires far greater skill and precision than drama. As Tallulah Bankhead put it: 'An onion can make you cry, but show me the vegetable that can make you laugh!'"[4] Certainly, the purpose of comedy, first and foremost, is to entertain, and, in some circumstances, to educate or inform, and Chan does both. Comedy is not easy to evaluate, as the more detailed the analysis, the less funny the humor. Early-20th-century philosopher Henri Bergson acknowledged this danger in his ruminations on the comic, describing his approach in an extended essay: "We shall not aim at imprisoning the comic spirit within a definition. We regard it, above all, as a living thing."[5] As popular comedian Steve Carell (*The 40 Year Old Virgin*, US television's *The Office*) remarks, "As soon as you try to deconstruct any sort of comedy, it's immediately not funny. It's just not like doing something serious, where there are these shades of meaning. With comedy, it makes people laugh or it doesn't. It's a Hail Mary in every way."[6] Comedy hides it artistry, so that the results seem spontaneous and natural. But to truly appreciate a film's craftsmanship, we must break it apart and consider how it comes to be funny, and whether the humor has meaning beyond the effect. As critics we can suck out the air if we over-analyze, and the film cannot breathe. So we will attempt to keep *He's a Woman* alive, first through classifying the film's comic structures, by turning to film historian Gerald Mast, and his eponymous study of the "comic mind" and then looking at how and what they mean.

Chan basically adapts (by picking and choosing) elements from four comic structures Mast identifies. In *He's a Woman*, the first of the four is "the familiar plot of New Comedy — the young lovers wed despite the obstacles (either within themselves or external) to the union. Boy meets girl; boy loses girl; boy gets girl."[7] Sam meets Wing, loses her, and regains her at the end. Chan adds cross-dressing and identity crisis and borrows from another structure Mast identifies as the *reductio ad absurdum* where "a simple human mistake or social question is magnified, reducing the action to chaos and the social question to absurdity ... . Perfect for revealing the ridiculousness of social or human attitudes, such a plot frequently serves a didactic function. After all, reduction to the absurd is a form of argument."[8] The logical fallacy of *reductio ad absurdum* contributes to the comedic effect. Chan's film focuses on the mistaken identity of Wing as male and gay, Sam's homophobia and identity crisis, and attitudes of Hong Kong society towards gays. Although Chan's movies are more loosely constructed, they are related to another structure Mast refers to as a "structural principle ... more leisurely, analytical, and discursive than the taut, unidirectional, rhythmically accelerating *reductio ad absurdum.* This structure might be described as an investigation of the workings of a particular society, comparing the responses of one social group or class with those of another, contrasting people's different responses to the same stimuli and similar responses to different stimuli. Such plots are usually multileveled, containing two, three, or even more parallel lines of action."[9] Here, not only are gender and sexual preference in Hong Kong society at issue, but class relations and social circles also. The distinction between ordinary people and celebrities are brought out through opportunities, lifestyles, and choices available to them. Lastly, Chan draws on "the story of the central figure who eventually discovers an error he has been committing in the course of his life ... The comic versions of the plot take place in a comic climate which is a function of who makes the discovery, what the discovery is, and what the consequences of the discovery are."[10] Sam's multiple discoveries, from fear of a gay encounter to tolerance of a gay protégé, from feeling a sexual attraction to a supposed gay man to reconsidering his own sexual desires with a resulting identity crisis, from acceptance of various genderings and wonderment that he has mistaken a woman for a man, provide comedy and pathos throughout the story. Chan's proclivity to blend comic structures is not unlike his pioneering development of the genre mix that has come to be known as the "dramedy," in which the comedic dominates but is supported and enhanced by genuine emotional sequences and serious consequences and themes.[11]

Still, Chan's movie shares proclivities with the Hollywood screwball comedy, with an emphasis on physical characterization, including body shape, facial expression, and gesture, as actors interact with objects of the mise en scène (think Wing in Sam's apartment) as well as episodic and wildly chaotic plotting rather than a continuous narrative, leading to social reconciliation and a happy ending; the leads (Sam and Wing) are characterized as opposites who eventually reconcile their differences. Chan borrows from two subgenres of the screwball comedy, identified by film critic Stanley Cavell[12] as the marriage (commitment) comedy and the remarriage (reaffirmation) comedy, as seen in the original film and its sequel, *Who's the Woman, Who's the Man (Golden Branch, Jade Leaf 2)/Gam ji yuk yip 2/Jin zhi yu ye 2* (1996), where at the inception, the couple do not recognize they are in love with each other, but eventually find each other, and, in the sequel, are separated and ultimately reunited.[13]

Chan mines humor in the everyday, and while it is a selective process, it appears as if discovered by accident, and the viewer, in Chan's company, experiences these apparently unexpected finds with him, delighting in their good fortune. Similarly, though, there are equally dramatic moments to be found in the everyday, and Chan's films share a wistfulness that is very affecting on an audience. *He's a Woman* could be described as a romantic comedy that follows not only the Hong Kong but Hollywood formula of "boy meets girl, boy gets girl, boy loses girl, boy gets girl, and they live happily ever after," except it adds not only the cross-dressing gender twist but genuine moments of empathy and pathos, making it something more. Hence, Chan delivers an emotional wallop, running the gamut from laughter to tears, by pioneering the "dramedy," a hybrid form that blends comedy with drama and pathos, discovering, as it unreels, the humor and heartbreak of life. The audience laughs with, not at, the characters (and sometimes cries, or at least feels for them) as the dramatic elements are incorporated. The "comedy" is infused with something "dramatic."[14] In fact, Chan draws on the rudiments of drama and plotting long ago described by Aristotle in *The Poetics*. There is complication and conflict, created through the cross-dressing aspects and Sam's characterization, a climax and even catharsis of sorts for some audiences (as the heterosexual romance of Wing and Sam is reified). Overplayed, the sentiment in Chan's films would be maudlin, but with the right touch it is fragile and effervescent. The reviewer known as Kozo, at "Love Hong Kong Film," describes *He's a Woman* as having a "glossy, Golden Age of Hollywood feel, and the story manages to be affecting without being overbearing."[15]

Kozo credits the United Filmmakers Organization with its "ability to handle comedy and drama in a light, sophisticated way."[16] In the tradition of other UFO films generally and Chan films particularly, we find an urban setting, with urban youthful characters, urban problems, and urban perplexities, treated in serio-comic fashion. Chan's distinctive sensibility grows from his vision of the world — that his stories could take place (and would be understood) in any global city, barring the language barrier. His urban youth, in films ranging from *Tom, Dick and Hairy (Three World-Weary Heroes)/Fung chan saam hap/Feng chen san xia* (1993), *He Ain't Heavy, He's My Father (New Two of a Kind)/San naam hing naan dai/Xin nan xiong nan di* (1993), *Comrades, Almost a Love Story/Tim mat mat/Tian mi mi* (1996), and *He's a Woman* weave stories about growing up and taking on responsibilities, and in all these films, sexual matters play a part. The virtue of Chan's filmmaking is the evolution of his characters through poignant and sweet stories of love, yearning, and relationships; characters keep missing each other, waiting for each other, and eventually finding each other, with Chan capturing the subtlety of those relationships and feelings, mixing both emotionally deep and over-the-top hilarious scenes.[17] He told film reviewer Betsy Sherman he likes to "maneuver emotions ... to make an audience laugh and cry ... to be thrown up in the air then dumped."[18] As an avid film-watcher himself, he explained, he likes to experience that thrill as well.

More broadly, Chan's genre-bending cinema reflects Hong Kong as a hybrid city, blending old and new in an original way.[19] Like Hong Kong making and remaking itself within its architectural, post-colonial, and triadic space, Chan draws upon the Chinese cultural past and Hong Kong's film past, not only citing history and culture but borrowing from the melodrama popular in Cantonese and Mandarin dialect films of the 1950s.[20] One melodramatic stock element, according to Ng Ho, is the pattern of the changing of roles,[21] in Chan's movie represented by the gender-bending of the plotting, for starters, and elaborated in a melodramatic tension, torn between comedy and pathos with character foils and contrasting lifestyles. Clowning, exaggerated facial expressions, and body language can be traced to the clowns of Chinese opera, as well as the coincidences that arise. But there are also moments of sadness, and the contrast between the comic and dramatic allows us to make connections, draw parallels, perceive ironies and contradictions, and explore themes raised by the story. This movie is more than simple escapism. The issues of gender, sexual orientation, and commerce Chan explores behind the humor and dramatics are serious in nature and lend themselves to closer examination, as explored in the following chapters. Indeed, Stephen Teo notes, "The genre of comedy relies on the rendering of a paradox on which humor is the mainspring to achieve a significant reading of the 'Other,'"[22] in this case a mainstream film in which the "other" is gayness.

What makes us laugh, as human beings? Philosophers, psychologists, sociologists, and cognitive researchers have all examined this question, from Aristotle to Kant, from Descartes to Freud. Laughter authority John Morreall notes the necessary conditions for laughter generally agreed upon: feelings of superiority; relief, as a release of tension; our perception of an incongruity; and/or the involvement of a sense of play or playfulness.[23] There are no universals, in terms of who laughs at what — "one man's (woman's?) meat is another's poison." According to Mast, in filmmaking, it is "a matter of rhythm and emphasis,"[24] an impression understood on the part of a director. Bergson reminds us that "to understand laughter, we must put it back into its natural environment, which is society, and above all must we determine the utility of its function, which is a social one ... It must have a *social* signification."[25] Bergson also notes the disinterested stance required by comedy, an intelligent perspective, at a remove from emotions. In our examination of the comedic elements, we will keep Bergson and Mast in mind, putting the film in a social context and examining its artistry, but since *He's a Woman* is both comedic and dramatic, we must also consider the audience's emotional response. What makes us empathize? Like pornography, as the US Supreme Court has decided, we know it when we see it. Mast continues, "Laughter is itself a physical-emotional response produced by intellectual recognition. The intellectual basis of comedy's emotional effect (laughter) is precisely what gives it its power as an intellectual tool."[26] I would suggest the same case could be made for drama; sometimes we are sickened by an emotional reaction, and thereby forced to confront it. In film dramedy, we know it when we feel it, we cannot deny it, it erupts over us and we respond to it, we cannot suppress it. While comedy dispels fear and offers relief, empathy makes us feel and think. As human beings living in the 21st century, we are bombarded with manufactured images on a scale never before imagined, and thereby are conditioned to read them; the power of filmmaking results not just from those making films or those writing about them, but also from those watching them and playing them in their heads. Film has always been and remains a collaborative and popular art form.

The Chinese proverb, "*Cheng xian qi hou*" translates as "to serve as a link between the past and the future" and refers to the undertaking of studies and enterprises.[27] I borrow it here to describe Chan's invoking a rich cinematic history, drawing on Cantonese and Mandarin comedy, particularly films of the 1950s and 60s, including the approximately 600 Cantonese comedies made during this time frame,[28] although those films originated in the Shanghai comedies of the 1920s and 30s. Cantonese comedies of the 1950s relied on comic dialogue, including nonsense verse, rhymes, and puns, as well as gags, according to Law Kar.[29] Law notes an "eclectic and inconsistent style" in 1950s and 60s Cantonese comedies and a "sensitiv[ity] to changes in society ... free from the bondage of established codes"; he also recognizes Hong Kong as possessing a "unique" society.[30] Released in 1994, *He's a Woman* capitalized on an international trend towards androgyny in the entertainment industry and popular culture as well as changing mores regarding gendering and sexual orientation, and the movie zeroed in on the local fanzine peculiar to Hong Kong popular culture.

Ng Ho's preliminary analysis of Cantonese comedy plots identifies many elements from which Chan borrows, including those from social satires and romantic comedies.[31] From the social satires Chan draws on those in which the "'little guys' [are] trying every possible means to make a living and dreaming of an abundant life," where people with their own individual problems share a living space (the pattern of *The House of 72 Tenants*), accidental acquisition leading to blunders and a moral lesson (the pattern of the sweepstakes craze), and a character "gain[ing] admittance into another social stratum" (the pattern of the country bumpkin goes to town). From the romantic comedies Chan makes use of the war between a male and female within an interior space (the pattern of the dividing wall), disguised identity, and the changing of roles, specifically, the assumption of roles of the opposite sex, and the house husband (traditional male-female roles are exchanged; this element appears chiefly in the sequel to *He's a Woman, She's a Man*).[32] Born in Hong Kong, Chan's formative years were spent there; his family did not move to Thailand until Chan was 12, and there he studied in an American high school. While I am not suggesting a direct influence, I am positing Chan's familiarity with the genre, and an exemplary Cantonese comedy of the tradition Chan follows is Chiang Wai-kwong's *First Come, First Served/Jie Zu Xian De* (1953).

Briefly, the slim plot follows a woman, Wong Sheung (Leung Mo-sheung) who injures her fiancé and flees to the city where she disguises herself as a male to find work. Helped by a radio host (Law Yim-hing), she becomes a successful singer as well as wins the heart of a male singer, Cheung Chin-chung. Many similarities between this movie and Chan's arise. The female lead is a girl from the countryside (as Wing is an "ordinary person"); both plots involve money problems of working class people, as distinguished from the wealthy. Both females are given spunky characterizations. Both films include lots of songs as well as comical auditions and unmasking of the female disguised as male. And both movies include female characters who mistake the female-disguised-as-male and pursue them as partners. *First Come, First Served* actually involves a five-sided complexity whereas Chan's film involves a triangle. The radio show host is pursued by Cheung Sing-bun, the buddy of the male singer, and the male singer's former girlfriend, Chow Yuk-lan, returns to pursue her lover. All's well that ends well as the couples sort themselves out (the cross-dressed female with her fiancée; the male singer with his former girlfriend; and the radio host with the male singer's buddy).

Chan's use of Cantonese idiom and slang goes back to the "Broker La" comedies of writer Gao Xiong and director Mo Kangshi, as noted by Law Kar.[33] But, unlike the earlier Cantonese comedies whose "plot structure was loose and episodic," and which lacked "a coherent vision,"[34] Chan's plotting is taut and the story structurally unified, dependent on character contrasts and a love triangle, and offering a consistent thematic view. Cheng also describes 1950s–60s Cantonese comedies as "moralistic and conservative and lacking a sense of satire and protest" and Chan's film in these instances is liberal and lightly satirical.[35] Interestingly, Cheng observes that the "Cantonese comedies refrained from expounding the prevalent male chauvinist ideology" and notes "their creation of quite a few unbending female characters,"[36] far ahead of their 1980s counterparts, citing films such as *A Comet of Laughter Lands on Earth* (1952), *One Queen and Three Kings* (1963), *Secrets of Marriage* (1965), and *Man of the House* (1967), among others. Characters like Wing and Rose in the original film and Anita Mui's

Fan Fan in the sequel follow such prototypes. Both the film's Chinese title and its opening sequence are signposts for a women's world. *Gold Branch Jade Leaf*, the literal Chinese title, is a common term used to describe Chinese female aristocracy of the past,[37] used here to refer to the power of the women in the story, namely Rose and Wing, and pointing to Chan's intentions in the film. He expected audiences to identify with Rose, to find Sam self-centered and selfish, and to see Wing as his next conquest — albeit behind the scenes, in a "reign behind the curtain," it is the female characters who orchestrate the plot developments. (The film's English title comes from a line of dialogue, "he's a woman," ironically referring in the story to Wing, but in the title referring to Sam's sensitive nature.)

Story and structure come first and foremost, because without a funny script and humorous episodes, no matter how great the cinematography, editing, and acting, it will fail to provoke amusement, and without a narrative arc, emotional impact will be lacking. Casting and delivery on the part of the actors, as well as their comic timing, and contributions made by the editor, musical composer, and filmmaker's vision, all play a significant role in this dramedy, with the humor enlivening as well as problematizing its gendered subjects. Director Ridley Scott, known primarily for his drama and action films, confesses: "As I go on, I'm very attracted to comedy. At the end of the day, because you've been having a good old laugh, you go home laughing — as opposed to dealing with blood all day and you go home and want to cut your wrists."[38] *He's a Woman* offers a good laugh and something more. As one spectator observes, "You don't have to be from a certain country to enjoy a good laugh. The fact that the movie is funny makes it an international film, crossing borders."

2

Camera, Sound, and Music

"Align your mouth, move to the right, move to the left, move right, move left, move up, move down, open wide and sing with passion." — Singing Coach to Wing, *He's a Woman, She's a Man*.

Comedy often hides its artistry, and this chapter attempts to reveal it. Credit goes to Chan's collaborators, director of photography Joe Chan Jun-git, editor Chan Kei-hop, screenwriters James Yuen Sai-sang and Lee Chi-ngai, composers Clarence Hui Yuen and Chiu Tsang-hei, and lyricist Lam Chik, as well as production designers Hai Chung-man and Lau Man-wa and costume designer Dora Ng Lei-lo, with most of the team reuniting for the sequel, *Who's the Woman?*. Chan has always recognized the collaborative nature of filmmaking, as evidenced by his partnership in UFO (United Filmmakers Organization), a collective of directors, writers, actors, and producers who came together and equally contributed to each other's films. *He's a Woman, She's a Man* became one of its critical and commercial successes. The story, conceived by Chan and UFO partners Lee Chi-ngai and James Yuen Sai-sang, is not, like *Comrades*, set against larger world events or dramatic happenings for its background; its grounding is the crazy world of the entertainment industry, the paparazzi, and fandom. In a sense, this makes the film more dependent upon sharply drawn characterization and the telling of more insular stories.

Film is primarily a visual medium, and its rich visual language is dependent upon mise en scène and editing. The former, composition within the frame, expresses the essence of a scene and includes not only the manipulation of people and objects, but the distinction of what the camera shows us versus what an unassisted human eye would see. Not only are the photography and lighting of camerawork (including perspective, depth of field, angle, and type of shot) integral to the mise en scène, but also blocking and movement, set dressing, costumes, and make up. The lighting typically gives the setting a feel for the time of day as well as establishes mood. More shallow depth of field is used to attract attention to individual characters or objects pivotal to a scene. Crane shots are used for establishing shots or dramatic emphasis, and Chan normally gets two days' use of the crane on a month-shoot.[1]

Chan is discriminating in the effect of his choice for camerawork, ranging from comic to dramatic. An active camera comically corners Sam (as does Rose) into signing Wing as a singer. On the other hand, several complex mirror shots reveal Rose's character, and, as Chan intended, create drama and audience sympathy for her. One of these shots features a full-length so-called "trick" mirror, the one in which Rose views herself before going public to insure her confidence (a comment on projecting image). The other is a smaller dresser mirror into which Rose peers, associated with the love card that Sam has given her (which plays "Amore"). One spectator, identifying primarily with Rose, commented this latter shot "worked wonders" for her.

While Chan occasionally uses some crane shots in the film, such as breathlessly pulling out and up (as Wing practices her singing on the office rooftop, revealing a generic, cosmopolitan cityscape), he favors the close-up to reveal character and emotion, medium two shots and shot-reverse-shots to develop relationships, and top shots to establish scenes. However, unlike many filmmakers today, he does not overuse the close-up to make it essentially meaningless, but carefully chooses close-ups at climactic moments. Sometimes the action or psychologically heightened moments are at a distance, requiring the viewer to stretch towards the screen, to learn more. The close-ups stand out because they are set apart from many medium and long shots. While leaving his actors room to explore in order to nurture spontaneity, Chan is known for giving actors specific instructions regarding their facial expressions, which are duly captured in the close-ups. To assure spontaneity, he averages no more than seven or eight takes.[2]

Editing, or the selection and arrangement of shots, is built with dramatic and emotional emphasis in mind, rather than to structure physical action alone, and generally mimics the invisibility of continuity editing, not only establishing verisimilitude and coherence, but functionally condensing the action. Chan's edit is generally fluid and non-obtrusive, with cross cutting and selective jump cuts used occasionally to contrast the quotidian existence of ordinary people with the presumably glamorous lives of celebrities, the desires of mismatched couples, and shifting relationships. The rhythmic pattern of the editing coincides with the musical cadences of the soundtrack, as in the audition montage. A meaningful cross-cut scene occurs as Sam and Wing collaborate at the grand piano in Sam's apartment, when Sam, inspired by Wing's simple tune, composes the movie's theme song. As he plays and sings, the camera cuts between the couple at the piano with Rose almost in tears in close-up overhearing the music in her apartment below. Not only is the physical distance between the couple and Rose evident, but the growing emotional distance between them. Rose begins to realize that she might be losing Sam (and it is at such a moment that Chan's intention that Rose is the protagonist with whom audiences identify is apparent).

Chan is certainly aware of how to meaningfully vary his editing style. For instance, four distinct rhythms are established through the editing in four scenes, each two paired by using a similar editing style but serving different purposes. In the initial audition scene, a montage of various types of performers (musically, stylistically, physically, and culturally) appears, accompanied by each one's performance (as well as classical music) to register the local, cosmopolitan, and global reach of Hong Kong pop culture. And it not only is comic, but provides wry commentary on the routine of image making. Secondly, intercut is the scene in Wing and Yu Lo's apartment, with Wing basically auditioning being a male, in various stereotypical costumes, for Yu Lo, also to comedic effect, but the cuts are much quicker, amping up the effect, and the purpose is to provide iconic and ironic gender commentary. Similarly, two scenes use cross cutting to different purposes. In the scene mentioned earlier above, the cross cutting between Sam and Wing at the piano (at their first touch) is contrasted with Rose overhearing Sam's renewed inspiration, the dramatic effect showing the growing distance between Rose and Sam, and the developing closeness between Sam and Wing. Another cross cutting penultimate scene shows Wing running through the streets to find Sam, and Sam isolated at Rose's party, building tension and drama.

Parallel shots and scenes are used to pattern the film. Sam overhearing the duet of Rose and Wing is counterpointed by Rose overhearing Sam and Wing composing at the piano. Wing overhearing Sam and Rose's lovemaking is matched by Sam overhearing the attempted seduction of Wing by Rose, and Wing reluctantly admitting s/he is gay. Furthermore, locations reappear to structure the action, sometimes as bookends to the story — an apartment party scene early in the film is replayed a year later at the end; Wing watches the music awards on a television with poor reception in her apartment at the film's beginning and end. Sam takes Wing to an upscale bistro for a tête-à-tête; Auntie, Sam's assistant and confidant (Eric Tsang) draws out Sam at the same table later.

Similarly, an up-and-down architecture is employed, from the upstairs-downstairs of Sam and Rose's apartment "layout" (with the male on top) to the above-and-below piano action that occurs in several scenes. Characters move upstairs and downstairs by the hidden passageway or the malfunctioning elevator, from apartment to apartment. Wing hides and is discovered by Sam underneath a studio grand piano (leading to their passionate kissing) and Sam finds the promiscuous Auntie with a new lover under his apartment baby grand. These up-and-down negotiations reinforce two of the film's issues. First, class distinctions, which are apparent throughout the film in many ways, contrasting the lives of ordinary, working class people versus wealthy celebrities, ultimately reinforce that people are people and share similar problems — Rose was once an ordinary person too (but she rejects returning to that "simple life"). Secondly, sexual orientation and gender issues are raised. Either characters directly "come out" — as when Wing confesses she is a woman, although Sam does not hear (there is a twist on outing) or characters dealing with homophobia (after discovering the lovers, Sam advises them to carry on, and admits "It's none of my fucking business").

For the most part, diegetic sound is employed, not only with the dialogue and sound effects, but even with some of the songs, since various auditions are overheard, and Sam and the old timers (with Wing as well at one point) perform the old Isley Brothers' song famously covered by the Beatles, "Twist and Shout." Exceptions include several non-diegetic jazz riffs that provide ironic commentary and the repeated musical themes associated with various characters and relationships, such as "The Innocent Girl," "Secret Glances," "Break Up/Rose and Sam," and the "Rose and Wing Theme," and a Cantonese cover and instrumental version of Dean Martin's "That's Amore," which announces the film's staked-out territory. The love-themed hit song "Chase" (a.k.a. "The Search of My Life") blurs the diegetic and non-diegetic distinction, as it is composed at the piano as part of the action within the film (diegetically), and later appears in the film in the climactic scene (non-diegetically); similarly, "Now and Forever" ("Sam's Theme") is initially introduced diegetically as Sam performs it for a bickering couple, and it reappears (non-diegetically) in relation to Sam's heartbreak. Classical western music, from Handel's "Hallelujah Chorus" from *The Messiah* and "Entrance of the Queen" from *Solomon* to Mozart's *Marriage of Figaro* is sampled non-diegetically to provide commentary and humor. Generally the music is used judiciously, with lots of piano to underscore emotional arcs.

The great Japanese director Ozu Yasujiro once commented that "The end of a film is its beginning"[3]; in other words, the elements judiciously selected and introduced at the start determine the narrative strategies that can anticipate the ending. The structural pattern imposed from the beginning on the story through plotting leads to its conclusion. Chan's film ends and begins with "That's Amore," and shows us the effects of love relationships in various permutations. How do we get to the final kiss and Sam's revelation "Male or female … I only know that I love you"? A classical plot paradigm (borrowed from Aristotle's suggestive study of classical drama structure, with exposition, rising action, and complication, leading to conflict, climax, and resolution) as well as visual and aural cues define the horizontal narrative development from one situation to another, one feeling to another. Retracing from the fireworks skywriting at the fairy tale ending back to the beginning, where a cockroach's point of view of an ordinary person's cluttered lifestyle and product placement accompanies the opening credits,

"That's Amore" links Wing to Sam; moving forward from the start to the union of Sam and Wing, each incidental scene contributes to this satisfying resolution, and the actors, in collaboration with the filmmaker and story, create realistic experiences onscreen to lead us to believe in its conclusion.

Although film primarily shows rather than tells, and the actors reveal character through their acting, including body language, physical movement, face and voice, the speech patterns of the dialogue also convey character. Sam's conversation as an articulate and intelligent music producer and creative writer is thoughtful, mature, and measured, but not without amusement and humor, and is sometimes peppered with obscenities to comical effect as he vents his frustration and sublimates his conflicts. Wing's slang and direct and simple speech expose her working-class sensibilities, her youth, inexperience and childlike naiveté, and her ordinariness, therefore making her a special person (as set against the superficial complications and meaninglessness of celebrity).

Settings and set decoration are kept to a minimum in the film, with interiors dominant, but they equally contribute. Working-class Wing and her womanizing but platonic roommate Yu Lo (Fish) (Jordan Chan) live in a cramped and cluttered one-room apartment that is contrasted with Sam and Rose's luxurious and spacious two-story flat, suggesting class distinctions; expensive furnishings and tasteful décor of the latter contrast with the former, and small details like the noticeable paintings of Tamara de Lempicka suggest the powers of desire and ambiguous sexuality (Lempicka was bisexual).[4] Sam's study becomes the sphere of masculinity as Rose's rooms reflect femininity, seduction, and female beauty. The unpredictable elevator (twice linked to Sam's complaining about exorbitant maintenance fees, hence another sign of economic class) that negotiates upstairs/downstairs becomes a site of contested terrain — the potential of upward mobility for Wing, closeted sexual repression for Sam, and the place to ultimately make a choice (no wonder Sam is claustrophobic). Public/private settings are also contrasted, that is, work (the office, studio, rehearsal rooms) with home. The remaining locations, from Auntie's exotic red-toned quarters (where Sam confronts his desires), to the chi-chi Indian restaurant Rose rents out for her tête-à-tête with Wing, and the upscale Peak restaurant Sam frequents, all serve functional and metaphoric purposes relating to class or gender. Costumes add to characterization, with Wing's transformation from a girl in overalls (similar to the child she shares screen time with early on) to androgynous unisex pantsuits as male singer and plainly white dressed young woman. Rose's womanly curves are emphasized by shapely gowns, Sam wears stylish but subdued and comfortable clothing, and Tsang's Auntie is garbed in swishy muu-muus. The montage of Wing's attempts at male self-fashioning (overseen by Yu Lo) is not only an hysterically funny send up of male stereotypes, but undercuts social constructions of masculinity.

Set decoration is meaningful, and the concrete objects and props used help move along the action (many props are incorporated into the action). They also not only have symbolic import, but ground the fantasy approach of the film (who has not dreamed of hanging out with celebrities they admire?) and its fantasy ending in reality. Consider the soft, feminine red roses (traditional symbols of love) that Sam brings home for an intimate dinner with Rose, used to connect the musical jam scene to the costume party following the music awards. Sam has given his buddy a rose for his wife, leaving him behind, and the next scene cuts to him entering the apartment, with the huge bouquet, to be accosted by the chaotic party scene. The roses, as other objects, also take on a personal and unconventional symbolism. Sam is allergic to roses, hence, an indicator of the current state of his relationship with Rose and a substitution for her. Roses reappear in Rose's apartment (feminized) and are also featured on the musical love card Sam has given Rose (traditional symbolism), which plays "That's Amore";

they die to signal the ending of their non-platonic relationship (personal symbolism) and the film's near end (foreshadowing). Similarly, the sculpture throughout Sam's apartment is used conventionally and more idiosyncratically. It is eye-catching and a sign of elite and expensive taste, but also phallic in nature, suggesting a stereotypical masculinity (and overcompensation, related to Sam's connecting manhood to sexual performance). Many other phallic objects appear, and are used humorously, from the ever-present light sticks (which determine some of the action due to misunderstanding) to the carrots and zucchini in the dining scene between Sam and Auntie.

Taken together, the various scenes, through their visual elements in tandem with music and juxtaposition, set the tone, as in the lovely elevator scene where Wing comforts Sam with light sticks and an ad-libbed dance and limerick; their growing friendship and romance is communicated as the camera moves in on their softly lit little world, and the Chan touch of a shooting star (unlike the canned Disney pixie dust), which magically appears as the tinkling of a xylophone (sounding like a child's toy piano), holds the moment, giving way to a melodic, rich piano. In contrast, when Sam attempts to run away from his problems, he is to be found alone and lonely, confused and depressed, in a desolate, flat room of washed-out colors, where Rose confronts him and their dialogue is arid and brief. A few musical bursts interrupt the silence of this emotional scene.

Undertaking a close read of some representative scenes demonstrates the artistry of the film techniques and illustrates the liberal politics of the film, as well as shows, according to some viewers, its shortcomings. The scenes move from looking, talking, and touching, to kissing.

Looking: The window scene occurs after Sam's assistant Jerry overhears Yu Lo helping Wing adjust her loose light stick, resulting in Jerry thinking they are a gay couple having sex in a toilet stall.

Besides the narrative plotting of the scene (to develop the gender misconceptions further and to expose Sam as homophobic), the mise en scène and montage significantly contribute to the humor. A double-paned window frames four figures, with the three assistants in the left window and Sam singly framed in the other. The outside scene consists of general point-of-view shots of what the group is looking at — Wing meeting Yu Lo outside the building for the first time after she has begun working for Sam and moved out of their small and crowded, working-class apartment. The scene cuts between Yu Lo and Wing, both expressing much physical enthusiasm and contact — Wing jumping into Yu Lo's arms, hugging him, sobbing — and at a distance the window ensemble and their reaction to what they are witnessing along with the narrative they give it comprise the short scene. With each cut back to the window, the camera moves in closer on its subjects, until finally a slow pan across from Sam's crew to Sam alone ends with an extreme close-up of a frowning Sam, warned to protect himself from a gay threat.

Talking: There is an immediate cut to the next scene I want to mention, set in Sam's study and designed to express masculinity. Dark paneling, leather chairs, Sam's father's fireplace, and book-laden shelves all reflect a male domain. Sam is positioned on a far plane in a corner, seated in a leather chair, reading, as Wing, riding her imaginary bike, peddles down the hallway and is invited in by Sam for a heart-to-heart. Sam confronts Wing regarding his/her sexual orientation in what can only be described as a self-reflexive moment for the reputedly bisexual Cheung himself. Cinematographer Joe Chan Jun-git keeps deep focus, from the foreground, where Wing is seated, to Sam, cornered in the background, with one rack focus shot at a crucial moment. With mostly two shots, over-the-shoulder and reverse shots, the camera slowly moves in on the scene, until both actors are featured in close-up and the scene turns very intimate. The dialogue is important, worth quoting at length, as Sam reluctantly pursues the gay question.[5]

Sam: Hey! Can you cycle in for a minute? Actually … I don't mind your private life. I understand that everyone has their privacy. But I have been suspecting something for awhile … I think we should be honest.

Wing: What do you want to know?

Sam: Are you … what?

Wing: What?

Sam: (frustrated) It's like this. Every business has its own rules. Just because I don't mind doesn't mean other people won't mind. Don't misunderstand me. I don't discriminate on this issue.

Wing: What are you saying?

Sam: Are you … gay?

Wing: I said No!

Sam: No?

Wing: I'm a bit sissy, but I'm 100% a man.

Sam: Okay, whatever. But I want to tell you that in the entertainment business, this is a very odd and sensitive issue. If you are, just don't let anyone see it.

The scene concludes with a comedic moment as both characters attempt to lock their broken doorknobs and sweat over being awakened in the night by the proverbial other. Sam twice denies his homophobia ("I don't mind") while he is obviously disturbed. One viewer likens the scene to a session between patient and therapist, but exactly who the patient is and who the therapist is could be debated.

Both of the above scenes ultimately play for comedy, and the in-joke, of course, is a sexually ambiguous man (in real life) playing a homophobic character that unwittingly falls in love with a woman he believes to be a man, and having to deal with an identity crisis and emotional turmoil. Still, Sam's characterization as homophobe, in this and other scenes, is contradicted throughout the film by Sam's strong and stable relationship with Auntie (Eric Tsang).

Tsang, one of Peter Chan's partners at UFO and a well-known staple on the Hong Kong film scene, as well as a former soccer player and father to a son-actor, plays a flaming, over-the-top gay stereotype for laughs. The polymorphous Auntie takes several lovers over the course of the film, but first and foremost he understands Sam better than Sam does himself. In fact, Chan explains Auntie as "the voice over. We needed to speak Sam's voice and heart out. We needed a character for him to springboard his ideas." Much of their interaction was unscripted and improvised while shooting.

Auntie serves as Sam's confidant and several scenes dramatize Auntie advising Sam; among them, the upscale restaurant scene atop the Peak where phallic imagery pervades the scene (again, to comic effect). When Sam, who thinks he is letting Auntie in on a secret, tells him, "he [referring to Wing] is really 'curly'" (slang for gay), Auntie, with a twinkle in his eye and an impish grin, replies, "I told you so." The scene opens with a close-up collage with cuts and pans of mouth-watering fruit pies and cheesecakes as well as the slicing of ripe tomatoes, crispy zucchini, squash, and carrots. Auntie flirts with a giant of an Anglo waiter with sparkling blue eyes, and a hilarious moment ensues as he points to the food with a fan, "I want this, this, this, and … this," as he aims at the waiter's penis. The shocked waiter flees while the camera tracks Sam and Auntie alongside a buffet, where three large protruding carrots stick out in front of Auntie, who grabs one and examines it during his explication:

> See? You can't force or push people. It needs time. I don't understand why you are afraid of him [again, referring to Wing]. He is so weak and skinny. You could even shake him off with your pinky finger. You people just don't understand our members' feelings. If we don't like women, then of course we like men. It's not like we like dogs! If we find someone we like, we should feel whether there's a reaction. Just like the commercial says, "Just do it!" If there's no reaction, don't bother. Too many men, don't waste my time.

A cut shows the two seated at a table, with the Central cityscape viewed out of large picture windows offering an elite distanced view of Hong Kong with strong natural light. The two are surrounded by mostly empty tables, and close-up shot-reverse shots play out the rest of the scene. Auntie continues:

> I suggest that you shouldn't lock your door. Open it! Because the problem is not his, it's yours. So ... are ... you ... gay?!

Editing, camerawork, and soundtrack simultaneously deliver the one-two punch here as a distance shot across the room jerkily, jaggedly (as if jolted by the line of dialogue), and seemingly haphazardly stumbles into Sam, ending in an extreme close-up as he nervously chews on his thumb and frowns, while an accompanying somewhat dissonant jazzy tenor saxophone delivers the K.O. (knock out punch). Talk about an identity crisis. The homophobic Sam has to admit he is attracted to another man (albeit, a childlike and androgynous woman disguised as a man). According to Chan, Sam reflects "the classic straight man's fear of gays — it stems from a fear you have from within. The guy's homophobic and freaked out because he's not sure who he is."

Touching: The first emphasis on touch[6] in the film occurs in the scene between Sam, Auntie, and Wing, as Auntie gives Sam his opinion on Wing's potential. Auntie approaches Wing from behind, lightly stroking his/her neck at the hairline. There is an extreme close-up, and the shot is held for effect to communicate the intimacy of the moment; in contrast, during the same scene there is a close-up of the loosened light sticks, suggesting an enormous erection, seen from Auntie's point of view in close-up; a close-up reaction shot of Auntie's surprise follows, and this moment, with no touch, is played strictly for laughs. A later scene pictures Wing and Sam at the piano, as she clumsily plays a few notes and he improvises the movie's theme song, "Chase." Seated next to Wing, Sam puts his arm over Wing's shoulder, and there is a close-up of his hand caressing the back of Wing's neck. When he realizes what he is so doing, he quickly withdraws his hand and literally jumps up in fright from the shared piano bench. Their next touch, at the office, in a piano studio, will lead to a passionate kiss.

Kissing: Kissing functions in both *He's a Woman* and its sequel to portray intimacy, and there are three significant kissing scenes in the original film. The first is set in Sam's study with a kiss between the Sesame Street puppets, the Count and Ernie, who are obvious stand-ins for Sam and Wing, who at this juncture cannot kiss; the puppets have been used to establish story and character, defining Wing as childlike and innocent and serving as her confidants. Here again, the close-up two shot, during which the personal relationship deepens between the characters, is played to comical effect as the puppets they have on their hands rise into the frame in a fevered kiss as the startled couple pull back, disturbed by their own desires, and the scene ends. Plot-wise, this scene is followed by Rose's departure on a trip, leaving Wing and Sam alone in the apartment together. Both avoid each other, and hence Wing flees the apartment, hiding under the studio grand piano, confiding in her beloved puppets, while the sophisticated Sam takes out his frustration on his old upright piano at home, only to show up at the office, inebriated, consoling himself with a bottle of wine. The scene, shot using a yellow filter, creates a golden glow and a potential imaginary space for the expression of their heretofore unrealized desire.

From Wing's perspective, a point-of-view shot shows only Sam's legs and the dangling wine bottle (phallic) he carries as he enters and seats himself at the piano, where he again bangs out his frustration. When the clumsy Wing hits her head underneath and the keys are struck, Sam peers beneath and as she attempts to escape he chases after him/her, pushes him/her against a wall and begins seducing him/her. "What do you want? No," she says. "Yes, we can," he replies. "I'm a man," she reminds him. "So am I," he responds. Their behavior reminiscent of animal mating rituals, they come closer, back off, come closer again in close-up two shots, leading to an intense kissing scene in which he throws her over the piano keys (allowing Chan to appropriate numerous filmic love clichés from the past), shown with a top shot in which they reverse positions (allowing women on top). Inter-cut with the piano insides as they literally "bang" away, the top shot reveals an extreme close-up of Sam's anguish as Wing continues caressing him and kissing his neck. He breaks away, "No! No!" and the scene concludes in a two shot with both characters standing, Sam in the foreground, Wing standing behind him at some distance, with Sam, speaking into the camera with his back turned to her, apologizing, "I'm sorry. You're not a woman," and exiting, as Wing murmurs to herself and us, "I ... am a woman."

The final kiss in this film takes place in the elevator, following Rose's party celebrating her success at the Hong Kong Music Awards. She and Sam have broken up, although they remain friends, and she has become her own woman. Several party scenes track her movement through the revelers, in her own element, while Sam is isolated as a distant observer. He returns to his apartment, and under his baby grand, a familiar sound encourages him to look for Wing under his piano. He is disappointed to find Auntie with his latest conquest, but this time his response is, "Sorry, carry on" and there is a close-up of Sam walking away from them and into the camera as he confesses, "It's none of my fucking business." A reverse shot shows him at the elevator doors with his back to us and the doors open to reveal Wing, as a woman, dressed in virginal white against the deep red walls. A cut to a close-up of Sam, amazed, is followed by a cut and reverse shot of Wing, telling him, "I am a woman," with a cut to his reaction, still staring in disbelief, followed by a cut back to Wing. "Really ... a real woman," she almost whispers. Sam walks into the frame and the remaining two shots unite them as a couple, with extreme close-ups as he takes her hand and they finally kiss as a heterosexual couple. He vows, "Male or female ... I only know that I love you." The elevator jams, but the claustrophobic Sam no longer cares, and as the screen fades to black, fireworks spell out "the end" as the Cantonese cover of "That's Amore" begins to play (allowing Chan to appropriate numerous Hollywood movie clichés for sexual consummation). While the credits roll, lights flash blue and red as the couple, in a medium distanced shot, keeps kissing and the song continues.

There is a definite thematic progression in the sequences analyzed above. From looking to talking, from talking to touching, from touching to kissing, the episodes build to the story's fairytale ending (and also the beginning for the sequel, which Chan had not at the time anticipated). First, there is the introduction of contingency, a theme common in Chan's oeuvre. Chance, accident, and fate, and the possibilities each raise in terms of human relations is something Chan questions in his movies. What Jerry has by chance overheard in the bathroom, mistakenly suspecting Wing is gay and sharing it with the crew, and what they are seeing rather than hearing leads to the comedy of the first scene as well as raises the gender issue. Secondly, Chan introduces proximity, and there is an actual physical development as characters begin far apart and move nearer and nearer to each other, ultimately with physical contact.[7] Third, the physical contact becomes more personal, intimate and intense. And fourth, for those audiences uncomfortable with gay sex, some of the dialogue as well as the physical actions become more threatening, while for some of those homophobic audiences, the techniques used in the film ease them into a broader perspective of toleration.

Gerald Mast reminds us, "What the director shoots, how he shoots and edits it, and how he underscores the pictures for the ear establish the way an audience responds ... So does the director's handling of camera angle, editing, lighting, and sound. Are the shots close or distant? Does he shoot from below, from above, or at eye level? Is the lighting bright and even, or somberly tonal? Is the editing invisible or obtrusive, rapid or languid with dissolves? Is the sound track cheery, tense, contrapuntal, silent? There are no formulas as to what techniques and methods will or won't inevitably produce comic effects, but that the union and combination of lighting, camera angle, décor, editing, rhythm, music, etc. do shape the way we respond is undeniable."[8] With all of these elements in mind, Chan, with the contributions of his collaborators, fashions an entertaining, humorous, and heartwarming story, both comedy and drama.

3

Cross-Dressing, Gender-Bending, and Sexual Orientation

"You scratch too uptight. It should be scratching naturally without you knowing it. If you scratch too oddly, your light stick will drop out and that's a problem." — Yu Lo (Fish) to Wing, *He's a Woman, She's a Man*.

Comedy in *He's a Woman, She's a Man* is dependent on character, characterization, situation, and structure, and as Gerald Mast points out, the comic movie has something to say about the relationship between humans and society, either "uphold[ing] the values and assumptions of society, urging the comic character to reform his ways and conform to the societal expectations, or maintain[ing] that the anti-social behavior of the comic character is superior to societal norms."[1] While Mast presents an either/or situation, Chan's movie, as we shall see, has it both ways, both reifying and challenging heteronormative values. Depiction of gender and sexual orientation is central to Chan's film and deserves discussion and examination of its apparent social values. Gendering (that is, the social construction of male and female), including gender similarities and differences, how gender is constructed and deconstructed, how it is reproduced, interrogates, and challenges entrenched boundaries; the relation between body, self, desire, and other; and sexual orientation (the physical behaviors we choose to act upon) are all "touched" on in the film. Chan uses a transformative imaginative, the fairy tale movie, to explore gendered subjects and desire within a social context. In our discussion, we will use gender to refer to social construction, that is, what is conditioned and condoned by a heteronormative society; gay for male homosexuals, lesbian for female homosexuals, and queer for all sexual minorities, including gays, lesbians, bisexuals, transsexuals, and the transgendered.[2]

For the following analysis, this heterosexual (okay, straight female, hopefully not too narrow!) writer certainly wants to avoid the trappings of sexual tourism, while at the same time recognizing that queer pop culture cultivates and constructs community, and that the heterosexual Chan's movie is a mainstream film primarily constructed for the heterosexual gaze. To what extent does Chan's film make assumptions about and perpetuate stereotypes of the queer community? Certainly to be dissected will be how queer life is (mis)represented in this commercial film. In *The Location of Culture*, Homi K. Bhabba reminds us "in the *fin de siècle*, we find ourselves in the moment of transit where space and time cross to produce complex figures of difference and identity, past and present, inside and outside, inclusion and exclusion."[3] We will explore Chan's representation of figures of difference, and how they are included and/or excluded, and the result. But first, this crossroads where we find ourselves today has its own history and has been long in the making.

Cross-dressing generally and female cross-dressing in particular appear as a traditional element in Chinese opera, with an enduring history and powerful presence dating back to the 13th century, and centuries later echoed in opera and period films of the 20th century. Siu-leung Li, in the study *Cross-Dressing in Chinese Opera*, observes, "The history of Chinese opera can ... be instructively described as a series of narrative fragments of 'gender trouble' ... constituted in and through gender b(l)ending ... and epitomized in its commanding tradition of cross-dressing."[4] From Chinese theater's golden age during the Yuan (1271–1368) through the Ming (1368–1644) and Qing (1644–1911) Dynasties, cross-dressing featured prominently, in the latter periods through aristocratically supported private troupes as well as in the public theaters. The private troupes were primarily female, performing the Kunqu style (specializing in young male and young female roles), while men dominated in the public theaters, especially during the latter part of the 18th and through the 19th centuries. Li notes "the first fully developed Chinese theatre to emerge in the Yuan Dynasty favored female players and female cross-dressing."[5] Not only were females prominent, they mixed with male actors onstage, and audiences were mixed as well. With the rout of the Mongols and the return of the Han Chinese and the restoration of Confucian values, male and female actors as well as audiences were restricted from mixing; hence the rise of private and domestic female-dominated theaters. It would not be until the mid-1920s, after the fall of the dynasties, that public female presence re-emerged when the mostly female Zhejiang province regional Yueju opera became popular and successful.[6]

With the advent of cinema, the cross-dressing of onstage theater "crossed over" with role reversals onscreen. Ng Ho notes "The traditions of Cantonese comedy in the Hong Kong cinema have been shaped by numerous factors, for example, by Cantonese opera, where roles are often reversed with males playing roles designated to be female and vice versa."[7] Pang Chai-choi and Lin Li agree. "Actresses assuming male roles was a common phenomenon in Cantonese films, especially romantic comedies, of the period."[8] Furthermore, the assumption of roles of the opposite sex was not only a staple of Chinese opera tradition, but in canonical Western drama also. Gerald Mast refers to the "trans-sexual twists" going back to Shakespeare's *Twelfth Night* and *As You Like It*, the twisted "romantic platitude that beauty is in the eye of the beholder" in *A Midsummer's Night Dream*, and the irony that "the boy and girl do not know that they are the boy and girl" in *Much Ado About Nothing*, and that these motifs successfully transferred to onscreen comedies.[9] And Peter Chan, with eastern and western influences, is familiar with both traditions.

Gender-bending and cross-dressing have been a part of Hong Kong cinema since its inception, starting with *Zhuangzi Tests His Wife/Chuang Tsi Tests His Wife*, the first Hong Kong wholly produced short (1913), in which Lai Man-wai (Li Minwei) played the wife, and in too many films to mention, some drawing from history and myth, such as those of Hua Mulan, and other countless adaptations from Chinese opera, such as those featuring the Yam-Pak duo (Yam Kim-fai and Pak Suet-sin). These all shared acceptable conventions, while Hong Kong cinema, starting in the 1990s, introduced stories of gay, lesbian, and other orientations, including new waver Tsui Hark's *Swordsman* (*Siu ngo gong wu/Xiao ao jianghu*) series (1990–93) and *The Lovers* (*Leung chuk/Liang zhu*, 1994) and directors Ching Siu-tung and Stanley Kwan, providing women with more dominant and active roles in their films. These filmmakers not only began deconstructing the "male gaze" of cinema, but began deconstructing the socially constructed masculine fantasies of cinema and problematizing heterosexual essentialism.[10] Chan identifies Mulan (the historical Chinese female general), and "the lovers" (also known as the "butterfly lovers," based on a Chinese folk tale concerning an ill-fated couple who are denied their love by parents and society, but reincarnated as butterflies after their deaths, the subject of Tsui's *The Lovers*) as "the kind of stories a parent tells a kid."[11] The cross-dressing aspect of both history and film appears in Chan's movie, which Andrew Grossman described as one of two "big transvestite romance[s] of 1994, and the most successful one to push cross-dressing into contemporary times."[12]

Two complexities arise from these role reversals involving gender-bending and cross-dressing. First, a distinction should be made between the gender-bending/cross-dressing in the movies themselves and in the public lives of the actors. For example, the Yam-Pak duo performed male and female roles respectively onscreen in nearly 60 Cantonese opera films. Off-screen, they were also a couple. In *He's a Woman*, in character as Sam, Leslie Cheung plays homophobic while Anita Yuen cross-dresses as a male and is mistakenly perceived by other characters as gay. Off-screen Cheung reputedly acknowledged a gay relationship with a longtime partner in a 1997 concert, with an ensuing perception among many of his bisexuality. Feng Luo's analysis of the star's movie roles and concerts delineates a "most ambiguous intersexuality," but ultimately labels the person Leslie Cheung as "unisexual" based on the actor's choice of the unisex English name Leslie and from the actor's public interviews, the writer inferring that "through the state of mind in his movies, it's not hard to find the relationship, between his personal perspective of gender identity and roles on stage. It is art performance as well as life."[13] (Cheung's sexual orientation will be discussed further in this chapter and following.) But diegetic and extradiegetic elements of gender and sexuality and their blurring will complicate our analysis of *He's a Woman*. Cheung's counterpart, actor Anita Yuen, is heterosexual. Her characterization in the film, as cross-dressed Wing, however, raises the contradictory responses of audiences to male versus female cross-dressing, which is not symmetrical or equal. Females cross-dressed as males generally gain power (as does Wing in the story). Males cross-dressed as females are objects of ridicule (think Jack Lemon and Tony Curtis on the lam in Billy Wilder's *Some Like It Hot*, 1959).

Leslie Cheung himself speaks of this inequity in Stanley Kwan's documentary on gender in Chinese cinema, saying, "When a woman plays a man, everyone seems indulgent. But a man playing a woman is unacceptable ... It should be fairer. If they can accept a woman playing a man, then a man playing a woman should be okay too."[14]

Instead of "cross-dressing," Marjorie Garber uses "crossover," borrowing a term coined by scholars to describe the success of black rap music artists with white audiences in the mid- to late 1980s.[15] Perhaps the term is more appropriate because Garber's original usage epitomized the contested terrain of popular culture with shifts in the social construction of racial identity. Simply put, for our purposes, "crossing over" constructs and deconstructs gender identities, contests ideological power relations by challenging binary sexuality and homophobic taboos, and introduces sexual desire. Rebecca Bell-Metereau notes "instances of cross-dressing or sexual role reversal are particularly effective in demonstrating the murkiness of gender distinction."[16] And such is the case in Chan's pair of films. Through laughter and comedy Chan lays bare the ideological codes buried by representation. Through dramatic elements, expressed by the feelings stirred, in both characters and audience, he nuances the emotional register and seriously questions heteronormativity and introduces sexual ambiguity as an option. From the stereotypical extremes of the womanizing Yu Lo (Fish) to the flaming and promiscuous Auntie; from the transformation of Wing from tomboy into popular androgynous male star to plain and virginal female; from the stereotypical gendering of spaces in the film's settings; and, from the gentle parody of ambiguous and repressed desires and inhibitions in the comical sexual scenes between Rose and Wing (Wing is transfixed by Rose's womanly body), paralleled by the comical sexual scene between Rose and Sam (for Sam to prove his manhood), Chan explores sexual proscriptions and prohibitions and provides alternative identities and emotional androgynies. By further raising the specter of homophobia, Chan emancipates genders held captive, initially through the cross-dressing (and resulting "cross-over") of Wing and the reactions of other characters to her, but substantively through the "crossing over" characterization of Sam.[17] The filmmaker comments not only upon gender identity (representing the instability of gender performativity) but upon sexual orientation and choice.

Chan's starting point for the film arose from mistaken gender identity. Chan, who wears his hair long, has sometimes been mistaken as a woman when seen from behind. He relates the following experience: "It's a very Asian thing, because Asian men and women have less physical differences than Caucasians. We don't have hair on our chests. A lot of us don't even grow beards, we need to shave a little bit, a moustache, there's nothing. We're not really hairy people. Our physical builds, our heights are not that different. Our skin is very soft. A lot of Asian men's skin is as soft as a woman's. It's sometimes very intimidating. For example, I have long hair. People walk behind me, they think I'm a girl ... Then, when a bigger man taps you on the shoulder like a buddy, and all of a sudden it's almost like a guy tapping on a woman's shoulder ... people think you're something, you're somebody else. Those are the kinds of fears Asian men have and I'm just trying to build it into the scene ... A lot of my friends share those views. We just don't talk about it."

Stereotypes abound in *He's a Woman* but are undermined as they essentially play for comedy, with an ironic self-reflexive commentary on stereotyping.[18] Chan contrasts the condoned stereotypes of heteronormative society with a more personal and humanized response, based on the dramatic aspects of the characterizations, and that the actors in the film play against type, from Leslie Cheung playing sexist and homophobic to Eric Tsang playing gay and promiscuous. Tsang's performance was so over the top that for many heterosexual audiences, it becomes caricature.

On the other hand, with queer spectators, the portrayal was perceived as even anti-gay.[19] The performance element by this handful of Hong Kong actors was not missed by fans (that fact provides additional insight into the world of Hong Kong entertainment and fandom, another thematic element of the movie). A heterosexual avid Hong Kong film-goer remarks, "The role setting was sort of a twist to the performers' personal images ... Leslie was known to be gay, and he was playing homophobic. Eric Tsang was a renowned playboy (as in Wong Jing's movies), Anita Yuen was dating Cheung Chi-lam, while Law Kar-ying was courting Lisa Wong. And they all played homosexual. That's why the gender confusion thing works especially well for the local audience." We should note here that the strategy used by the filmmakers is inoculation, a recognized rhetorical device.[20] By providing the opposition (in this case, potential homophobic viewers) with a weakened version of the values held in opposition to one's own (in this case, the filmmakers), especially when emotions are involved, the opposition response proves less hostile. In Chan's film, Tsang's performance serves as a shot in the arm that allows the opposition audience to laugh rather than be disgusted (and maybe learn something to boot). In fact, one viewer stated, "I don't believe there is any gay stereotyping, or at least I didn't notice any," adding that Chan's message is that "people should not judge a book by its cover ... Everyone needs to find what makes them happy, no matter what it is or how people view it."

Performance aspects appear in relation to *He's a Woman* in several and varied areas. First are the characters in a film narrative performing gender, cross-dressing, and gender confusion. Second is the casting of actors/stars and the baggage of their public images and reception, specifically in relation to gender and sexual orientation, which circles back to affect audience perception of the characters in the film (with several in-jokes for knowing fans). And, third is the presence of actors living their personal lives, sometimes publicly, again bleeding into public acknowledgement. Judith Butler emphasizes the social and cultural construction of gender, which she defines as performative, developing over time through stylized repetition.[21] She stresses the role of repetition, with performance not as a singular act but as ritualized production, which can be reiterated under prohibitive and tabooed conditions. In *He's a Woman*, therefore, the performative element is virtually nonexistent, undercut first because the actors are simply performers performing in a movie, playing their roles, distinct from their real selves. And this performance is doubled as a character such as Wing is simply and temporarily performing as a cross-dresser. This type of performance is not far afield from the performances we all put on as we try out and adjust to the norms of a heterosexual hegemony, no matter our gender identity or sexual orientation. Cross-dressing in the movie can be understood as one in which various personae are tried, only to be discarded, with Chan nailing stereotypical heterosexual codes. Take, for example, the montage in mostly medium two shot of Wing and Yu Lo, as he instructs her on how to be a man. It not only presents stereotypical constructions of masculinity (via an assortment of macho costuming), at which even homophobic audiences laugh (inoculation) but puts an emphasis on phallocentrism (her lack of a penis and the need for one) and acceptable male behavior ("walk, walk, scratch scratch"). However, an uninoculated gay Hong Kong viewer described this scene, where Yu Lo tells Wing all men feel "itchy" and must scratch, as "vulgar."

Still, for the majority of audiences surveyed in this study, the references to Michael Jackson's androgyny and the use of light sticks added a stroke of hilarious genius — conflating how acceptable masculinity and androgyny is sold and introducing the factual world of fandom for music and film stars (whereas in the US, concert-goers flick their lighters for encores at concerts, Hong Kong fans wave light sticks. At some Cheung concerts, fans would spell out "Leslie" with them. That is dedication.) Wing's self-consciousness, introduced here, reappears throughout the film as she, for better or worse, attempts to convince according to the part she has created — as effeminate male and singer. As Mast points out, "The manipulation of physical business, so important to an art that depends on the visual and, hence, physical, provides one of the important clues about a film's emotional climate."[22] The physical action, from the popping up of light sticks to gawky dance imitation, is supported by key emotional moments, such as Wing's diffidence, from misremembering lyrics or improvising her back story, which furthermore distinguish between the stereotyping and the more human tenor of the story. For instance, when Sam asks Wing about his/her childhood, Wing cites the memory of playing house as a child, which Sam (and conventional society) deems inappropriate for a man. Through a quick conversation, Chan not only shows Wing desperately "winging" it, often backtracking to explain him/herself, but also notes the general sexist attitudes of society.[23] Wing's performance, with some missteps, furthermore makes the distinction between performing gender and performative gendering, and at the film's end, she appears dressed as a woman, when "a woman is a woman," in some respects, Sam is unconvinced ("It doesn't matter whether you are a man or a woman ..."). This distinction affects the film tonally, allowing for oppositional audience inoculation while exploring gender and sexuality in a non-threatening way for homophobic viewers. At the same time, it is a nod towards the uninoculated homosexual viewer perspective cited above.

Furthermore, the masculinity montage undercuts stereotyping and reifies the necessity of reiterated ritualized acts over time as a condition of gendering as performativity, if one accepts Butler's proscription of gender. In contrast to the film, performativity as a condition of gendering is readily apparent in the case of real-life actor Leslie Cheung. As Luo notes, Cheung's performativity in his preference and performances in film roles, in interview, and onstage (in concert) and off,[24] would ultimately define his gender and sexual orientation as well as cause cognitive dissonance for some audiences and fans. The conflation and contradictions between film and real life appear below, specifically in relation to Cheung.

Meantime, in the film, as Wing's cross-dressing and its complications make the gender theme visual and obvious, her representation and sexual positioning, although the lynchpin for the plot, is fairly straightforward.[25] She knows she is a heterosexual female (only temporarily befuddled by her attraction to Rose's womanly curves) wearing a disguise, never projecting a self-concept as lesbian, transvestite, transgendered, or other than who she plainly is, "an ordinary person." Similarly, Rose never sees a challenge to her gender or sexual orientation, even when she is attracted to Wing but discovers he/she is supposedly gay, and when she finds out Wing is female, she merely sees the ingénue as her sexual competitor for Sam. Both women, however, exhibit "normal" sexual desire and curiosity. With Sam, however, Chan fashions a much more complex and subtle examination of gender identity and sense of self, as well as a marginalized sexuality, unusual for a mainstream movie. Sam's homophobia and overcoming of the prejudice would have been an adequate plotting device for most comedies; here, however, Chan makes the focus Sam's gender identity, sexual desire, and confused sense of self, the story developing as a result of the permutations of his feelings and thinking and actions, and the story's arc turning ultimately on his transformation. He has fallen in love with a younger woman he believes to be a man, and we witness the shame and torment he endures because of his homophobia (a reverse of Balzac's titular character in *Sarasine*, in which a young man falls in love with a castrato, a man he believes to be an older woman) as well as his overcoming it and redefining himself. Bound up by his sense of manhood (especially heterosexual sexual performance and attraction) and need to control (previous singers he has produced, before Rose, Rose herself, and now Wing), Sam eventually relinquishes the latter need and rethinks the former, overcoming his fears and prejudices. Chan explains: "Sam's phobia is about himself, his sexual identity. Why are you so scared? All you have to say is no. Why are you afraid? You're not sure of who you are yourself. That's the point. Straight men's fear of gays stems from a fear from within." So the film manages not only to criticize traditional social conventions by crossing gender boundaries but also pokes fun at stereotypes by tapping into conscious and unconscious fears, desires, and prejudices.[26] With Sam, Chan targets the psyche of uptight heterosexual men pressured by social conventions that result in suppressing their feminine side, by offering a safe alternative identity by film's end. Sam enacts the strong, silent male stereotype until his indulged sexual fantasies about Wing loosen a few bricks in the wall of an overly deterministic male gender identity condoned by a heterosexual (and often homophobic) society.

We follow Sam's trajectory from supposed homophobe to his indifference to sexual preference; he understands love of any ilk — that is the value and message the film promotes. Even without journeying to his dreamed-of generic Africa (where he believes he will discover new musical inspiration and live a simpler life), through the events that transpire and his responses, he comes to a better understanding of who he is, of his relationships to others, and to a more tolerant perspective. Notably, his character disappears after the storyline's crisis — his failed lovemaking with Wing over the grand piano (while the comparison may seem unwarranted, it is provocative; in Shakespeare's *Hamlet*, we find a common pattern — just as Hamlet disappears for an entire act, to return a changed man[27]) — to be found by Rose a more mature person, one who seems to accept his current reality, whatever that may be, with no illusions about his relationship with Rose and determined on their breakup. To the contrary, the wishful Rose thinks that now Wing is out of the picture, she and Sam can continue their love affair (even though that connection was as much illusion as reality — people grow apart).

Following Sam's reaction to Auntie and his new conquest under the piano ("It's none of my fucking business") is his final "Male or female ... I love you," to Wing, two strong statements in the dialogue bringing about the story's resolution and asserting a belief in each to his/her own, tolerance, acceptance, and love. Andrew Grossman, however, sees this ending as "both moot and marginally hypocritical," claiming that Sam has just been assured that Wing is female before making his last love-affirming, poly-gender embracing statement, and further explaining that "the man falls in love with the woman *as* a man, as if a forbidden homosexuality were necessary to both activate and 'excite' otherwise banal heterosexual love."[28] A 20-year-old male bisexual viewer concurs: "It would have been much more romantic if Sam could have loved Wing even as a man, proving true that love is love and that such a force transcends skin and bones." A 26-year-old gay Hong Konger adds: "What I find memorable is its [the film's] failure to speak for/of queer ideologies — conversely, the opposite (e.g., stereotyping, homosexuality overpowered by heterosexuality) is displayed." While Chan certainly presents a heterosexual gaze and reifies the heterosexual relationship, I would point out that at the same time he does open the closet door and look inside, not before seen in mainstream Hong Kong movies circa 1994. And I would argue with Grossman's attribution. Is this love "banal"? It has been hard earned through the course of the film. Or does Grossman mean Wing's characterization as an "ordinary person" (as most of us are, whether straight, gay, bi, trans, or other) is "banal"? Or, is heterosexual love by definition as mainstream and acceptable, "banal"? Furthermore, Grossman neglects that moments earlier Sam has accepted the gay couple (Auntie with Joseph/Josephine) going at it under his piano, muttering, "It's none of my fucking business" [in English] as he walks away to leave them in privacy. Or, is there the possibility that members of a queer audience occasionally prefer to laugh their troubles away rather than deal directly with serious and painful homophobia in contemporary society?

Studies from theorist Michel Foucault to historian George Chauncey have documented that homosexuality as defined as sexual object choice is a modern European and late 19th- early 20th-century invention, with the invention of the homosexual character type appearing in literature, although homosexual acts have been documented historically.[29] It is furthermore ironic that "China in imperial times had relatively open and tolerant attitudes toward male and female same sex love.[30] Psychoanalyst Lionel Ovesey pioneered in the study of homosexuality in the 1960s with his study *Homosexuality and Pseudohomosexuality*,[31] in which he broadened the comprehension of psychological motivations, asserting that not only do people suffer anxiety over their sexual identity, but that heterosexuals with anxious tendencies display "pseudohomosexual" behavior (as in having same-sex sex) but are reluctant to be identified as "homosexual." In the aftermath of the Stonewall Riots of 1969, which ushered in the Gay Liberation movement, in the 1970s B. Ruby Rich's pieces in *The Village Voice* and Richard Dyer's edited collection of essays in *Gays and Film* initiated gay film studies and established a distinct voice integrating film aesthetics and identity and sexual politics.[32] By the early 1980s, Vito Russo's *The Celluloid Closet*[33] set the tone for much gay film analysis, providing an historical framework and gay point of view for studying Hollywood product. Film historian Richard Barrios's *Screened Out*[34] shows how Hollywood has depicted gays and lesbians onscreen and the mixed messages sent. *Queer Cinema: The Film Reader*[35] tackled gender, race, class, and age in its examination of queer cinema.

Recent scholarship in queer studies (or, in the current lingo, LGBT—lesbian, gay, bisexual, and/or transgendered) has focused on identity and sexual politics. Transgender studies like Judith Halberstam's *In a Queer Time and Place*, Jay Prosser's *Second Skins*, and Diana Fuss's *Identification Papers*,[36] have all advanced how we understand queer identity as detached from sexual identity. Judith Butler, in *Gender Trouble*, would question the naturalization of gendering and in *Bodies That Matter: On the Discursive Limits of "Sex*,"[37] would emphasize the performative element of gender identity, for people of all persuasions, its artifice, imitation, and chance elements. Many studies acknowledge Foucault's significant contribution to queer studies in his three-volume *The History of Sexuality*,[38] which represented both heterosexual and homosexual desire as constructed and reasserted the importance of history and socialization, also preventing essentialist interpretations of gender identity, recognizing that identity is fluid and subject to change. Such understanding can be seen in Gordon Brent Ingram's *Queers in Space: Communities, Public Spaces, Sites of Resistance*, whose approach Helen Hok-sze Leung uses to discuss the "queerscapes" of contemporary Hong Kong cinema to analyze how "public space is negotiated, reclaimed, and reinvented along the fault lines of heteronormative ideology."[39]

Leung points out the apolitical nature of most Hong Kongers,[40] with gay activists only recently adopting direct action, when in September 2000 gay organizations united to challenge legislative candidates on their attitudes towards sexual minorities, the first time the "pink vote" was visibly organized. In contrast to gay culture in the west, within the Hong Kong queer community ambivalences remain in regards to "coming out." Leung explains that traditional values shared by Hong Kong society prevail — including a defense of heterosexual marriage and family and filial piety. Because Hong Kong is a small place and physical space is valuable (with a large population, housing shortages, and impossibly high rents), many adults continue living with their parents or in close proximity. "Coming out" can be a traumatic experience, resulting in stigma and social ostracizing from family, friends, and acquaintances.[41] So much of the new queer scholarship (and much of it from the west) has literally spoken a foreign language to one of its potential communities, but that has begun to change since the decriminalization of homosexuality in Hong Kong in June of 1991.[42]

That change, however, has been gradual at best, taking place in fits and starts. Despite Leslie Cheung having, for all practical purposes, come out during concerts starting with the *World Tour '97*, he was still reluctant, in 1998, to discuss gay films (much less gay issues). In an interview conducted by June Lam for *City Entertainment*,[43] Cheung twice remarks, "This question is too sensitive," when asked first to compare the gay relationships in *Farewell, My Concubine* to *Happy Together*, and second, when asked about John Lone's character in David Cronenberg's *M. Butterfly* (1993), set during the Cultural Revolution and in which Lone played a Beijing Opera performer specializing in female roles against Jeremy Irons's French diplomat who falls for him, not at first realizing the actor is a man. (Cheung had been offered the role). Of *Farewell*, Cheung concluded, "The homosexuality theme is too sensitive ... In the 1980s, homosexuality is not opened up. I can't be a trendsetter. Right?" He added, "I don't play many gay films anymore, a modern one [*Happy Together*] and an ancient one [*Farewell, My Concubine*], it's enough." If even Cheung is uncomfortable discussing screen portrayals (not even real life), what specter does this raise for "ordinary people"?[44]

Closeting and coming out appear in both *He's a Woman* and its sequel, with the elevator in Sam's building substituting for the closet. Closet-like in its small, enclosed space, the elevator functions as a sign of Wing's upward mobility (see Chapter 4) but also serves as the site of Sam's identity crisis. Sam suffers from claustrophobia and each time the malfunctioning elevator is stuck, he desperately tries to escape its confines, panicked — cursing, screaming, and at one time cowering in a fetal position. He is uncomfortable in the elevator with Rose, but with Wing he learns how to cope (the omnipresent phallic light sticks assist, as Wing and Sam perform a Madonna-like dance duet while rhyming a tongue twister including Madonna's name). And the elevator serves as the set for the finale discussed above, and the culmination of Sam's long pent-up desire. Sam's coming out (or crossing over) is left, like identity itself, as somewhat ambiguous. But for the moment, at that time and place, identity and desire are revealed. And in some ways, reel and real life crossed.[45]

Although Cheung never officially "came out," according to the popular website "Love HK Film," "in every way imaginable, except officially, Leslie admitted to his homosexuality ... as it became known to all that he was gay, it still didn't matter — he was their own and they loved him."[46] Visualize the form-fitting boxers (that accentuate the male anatomy) and t-shirt (picturing a perfect but headless male nude, with an attached leaf covering the subject's member) that Rose selects for Sam's costume for the opening party in *He's a Woman*. The "costume" celebrates the male body and Leslie Cheung in it, a doubling of male stardom and star body, advertising a contemporary mediated masculinity, a new manhood. The body tells what, at least for Cheung personally, cannot be said. (It may be that Cheung remembered that costume, because during some of his final musical stage shows, he wore similar form-fitting black shorts.) Hong Kong concerts are reminiscent of Las Vegas stage shows, with a huge "wow" factor. They are professional and glitzy crowd-pleasers, very theatrical, bursting with special lighting effects and pyrotechnics, flamboyant and glittering costuming, with full orchestras and numerous dancers, exhibiting sophisticated and showy choreography.

In 1989, Cheung made history by selling out 33 nights of concerts ("Final Encounter of the Legend") at the Hong Kong

Coliseum. Cheung's shows, beginning with his "World Tour '97," promoting the release "Red" (12 December 1996–4 January 1997, with more than 50 concerts in Hong Kong and more than 30 internationally) and culminating with his "Passion Tour" (31 July 2000–16 April 2001, again, close to 50 concerts and venues in Hong Kong, Malaysia, Atlantic City, Las Vegas, and numerous cities in Mainland China, Japan, and Canada), gave new meaning to the entertainment form. For the "Red" tour, his costumes included brightly sequined suits and transparent shirts, he wore bright red lipstick and sparkling sequined high heels (which a male dancer lovingly strapped onto his feet during the show), and he performed some highly erotic dances with male and female partners. The "Passion" tour continued the trend, this time with Cheung wearing long skirts (the costumes were designed by Jean-Paul Gaultier) and waist-long straight hair down his shoulders and back (reminiscent of the old Cher, except for the wispy facial hair moustache and goatee). The concerts proved to be, if you will, Cheung's unspoken "coming out"/crossing over as well as demonstrated his understanding of eroticism and the erotic imagination.[47] For the "Red" concerts, the boyish Cheung also appeared in an impeccable and stylishly conservative tuxedo. As with Sam in his costume, and Cheung in his, how he presented his body in both cases combined fantasy and innocence, making audience awareness of desire (on the part of the viewer) and the presence of the desirous object (Leslie Cheung) something to contemplate. Sexual indeterminacy? Straight, gay, bisexual, transvestite, transexual? Choose your fantasy.[48] Furthermore, for a gay audience, Cheung cut a figure symbolic of gay pride. And how is queer spectatorship different from the heteronormative perspective? Travis S. K. Kong observes, "the question becomes not whether gay men find pleasure from the proliferation of gay images in Hong Kong films, but rather how one might read and understand such pleasure."[49] Certainly, queer viewpoints expand the vista for possible interpretations, challenging the master narrative of heteronormative ideology and allowing for more freeplay and possibility.

Peter Chan's winsome playfulness in *He's a Woman* led to more gender complexity and daring in the sequel. Even Grossman describes *Who's the Woman, Who's the Man?* "though less popular ... actually the richer and more complex of the two."[50] Chan introduced an independent lesbian character called O (Theresa Lee), comfortable with her identity and sexuality, and a serious relationship between Wing and another female singer, Fan Fan (Anita Mui), of ambiguous sexual orientation, but presumably a bisexual who has sex with both Sam and Wing. Yu Lo (Fish) reappears, desirous of the uninterested lesbian, as does Rose (Carina Lau in a cameo) as the shoulder for Wing to cry upon. Fan Fan occupies Rose's former apartment, and the movie opens with the concluding elevator scene from the first film and continues shortly with a costume party similar to the one in the first, also addressing some of the same territory in relation to the entertainment industry and celebrity. The sequel, however, despite its comic moments, is more serious in tone and raises more substantive questions about gender identity, sexual ambiguity and desire, and the price of fame.

During a private moment, Wing confides to Fan Fan, "It would be perfect if you and Sam were the same person" (gender blending), and extreme close-ups show the women, before a fireplace, in a near kiss interrupted by the ring of a doorbell (it is Sam). Once again, Chan deconstructs the male/female and straight/gay binary oppositions, but with the sequel, he goes further. As Wing and Fan Fan become more intimate, their feelings intensify and are revealed in a passionate lesbian kiss that occurs between the two women in the film-within-the film (shades of Truffaut's *Day for Night*). While the narrative has built to this moment, as Wing and Fan Fan have quietly shared private thoughts and feelings in a nurturing "female" realm, this scene, however, is anything but private. With an entire film crew to witness, the couple perform in a Chinese *Gone with the Wind*, with Mui cross-dressed as Rhett Butler (including the pencil-thin mustache) opposite Yuen's Scarlett O'Hara (and technically, since Wing is thought to be male, she is cross-dressed as well). Both women appear nervous, and a confident and cocky Sam observes on set as take after take is ruined. Despite the public and male setting (the women are surrounded by men and penetrative machinery) the sexual attraction between them is undeniable, and just as Sam was faced with a seemingly sexual identity crisis in the previous film, he is now confronted by the honest lovemaking of two women, both of whom he has slept with and one of whom he loves. As the camera slowly moves in on their expression of affection and desire, and cuts between them and Sam to reveal his shock, jealousy, and disbelief, he shouts out "cut" and flees the scene, captured in a top shot accompanied by melodramatic arpeggios. For many heterosexual audience members, Sam reflected their response.

Much of Sam's role in the sequel, *Who's the Woman?*, in fact, is gender-twisted as a typical female characterization — he is the stay-at-home waiting for his partner's return, he worries about fidelity, and he confides in Auntie. And if, as Chan points out, Auntie speaks for Sam, he is the symbolic visualization of the feminized Sam. Wing, meanwhile, is likewise twisted; she is career-oriented, stays out late, and has a carefree attitude regarding responsibility to nurturing their relationship. Both are unfaithful to the other, but Sam's unfaithfulness is dependent upon mistaken identity (at the costume party, both Wing and Fan Fan wear identical zebra-patterned costumes and Whoopi Goldberg masks) first, and sexual (and masculine) insecurity, second. Sam, in loose boxer shorts and undershirt, a nod to his muscled t-shirt and briefs in the first film, wears a Woody Allen mask (Chan's homage to a filmmaker he admires, but certainly a comment on male insecurity, self-doubt, and neuroses). Fear of sexual inadequacy is introduced, also reintroducing Sam's sexual hang-ups, as the masked Fan Fan offhandedly remarks to the masked Sam (unknowing that she is speaking to Sam) that everyone knows Sam Koo is gay, so he proves her wrong (actually, this brief scene is reminiscent of his comical lovemaking to Rose to the tunes of classical western opera, when he is also questioning his manhood). Wing's infidelity, in contrast, is predicated on the physical attraction and feelings of intimacy she experiences towards Fan Fan. The role reversal of Sam and Wing is indicated by the film's English title, questioning who plays which gender role. Subverting expected male-female relationship conduct reflects another way in which Chan toys with gender, and the couple's infidelities also reflect the reversal of conventional sexual roles. Indeed, both characters, in both films, experience growth and transformation in positive ways.

Grossman notes that in the sequel Sam "will regressively reassert the homophobia we thought the trials of the first film had dispelled ... Sam is afraid of being seen as a public gay couple [since Wing's fans believe her to be male]."[51] Grossman faults the character and story, but ignores the character's motivations — that is, Sam fears the censure of a homophobic society, what I would refer to as the gender uncanny, drawing on Freud,[52] when events repeat themselves in an eerily uncanny way. Something has happened to revive repressed, infantile feelings. For Sam, his repression involves his fear of commitment. And since of course this is a sequel, based on a very popular predecessor, Chan hits notes similar to the first film to satisfy his intended audience.

In addition to citing Sam's supposed reasserted homophobia, Grossman mentions the film-within-the-film kiss as a way to easily dismiss the transgressive conduct of Wing and Fan Fan as mere performance, and Chan himself for his denial of the film as about homosexuality. First, the performative *Gone with the Wind* kiss is part and parcel of the public acting out of two confused women simultaneously attracted to each other and in the first blush of love.

Second, as explained above, the scene emphasizes the effect on Sam, and it is a climactic moment in the film that leads to the turning point to follow — their female lovemaking, Sam's discovery of it, everything revealed all round, and Sam and Wing both growing up and reconciling, despite the messiness of life and relationships. How could the story be otherwise, when the Chinese sequel title remains the same, with the same star (Cheung) as lead? Regarding the director's intent, Chan relates: "I was struggling hard to make sense of the Anita Mui character. We were literally writing as we went, and I finally got the character nailed down three days before we wrapped, literally. Most of the film was shot by then. Part of the key to her character was an inspiration from *Citizen Kane* ... She'd found her 'rosebud' ... I never meant for it to be very sexual, their relationship. That's really about a young woman [Wing] ... She finally finds someone [Fan Fan] who really cares about her. It's a moment of connection between two human beings, whether they are men or women, and that's what it was supposed to be. But I couldn't find a way ... to express that without having a love scene ... It's not really about homosexuality ... The movie's about two people connecting at a very platonic level."

In a landmark study of poetry many years ago, William Empson described seven types of ambiguity,[53] two of which are appropriate to understand Chan's fence-sitting here. First is the "fortunate confusion ... when the author is discovering his ideas in the act of writing, or not holding it all in his mind at once."[54] Note that Chan describes the urgency of finishing the film, the necessity of having to use the footage already shot, and the lack of a satisfactory dramatic solution to express the relationship. Chance has always been an integral part of filmmaking. Second, Empson identifies as most ambiguous of all types the ambiguity "full of contradiction, show[ing] a fundamental division in the author's mind."[55] Chan has admitted discovering the politics of the first film along with his audience; in the second, despite his intention to avoid the lesbian subject, such development provides the lynchpin for understanding the intimate and heartfelt nonsexual relationship remaining between the two women. In Chan's remarks above, he sounds just like Sam at the end of the first film — it does not matter whether you are male or female, etc. Furthermore, Chan's disclaimer is not unlike the Marx Brothers denying social intent in their films or William Faulkner explaining he did not write about the South.[56] Grossman ignores the fact that not only does Chan make mainstream films, but the "bent" of Hong Kong movies, with few exceptions, is commercial. The Hong Kong film industry, first and foremost, has always been commercially driven.

Grossman describes Wing and Fan Fan as "vengefully defying Sam's scheming" and further criticizes the film and Chan: "Their [Wing and Fan Fan] actualized lesbianism *finally* breaks diegetic cross-dressing's limitation of sexual bounds, transgressing the generic separation of homosexual form from heterosexual content ... But, frustratingly, director Chan will not allow them to enjoy their lesbian transgression for even a moment ... . Even its [the film's] boldest transgression is only a play-act without sociopolitical merit — ... it winds up negating sex instead of liberating it."[57] Disturbing here is that Grossman inadvertently characterizes lesbian behavior as vengeful, a position more negative than the one for which he criticizes Chan.

Another way of understanding the motivation, in particular regarding Mui's character, is that with Fan Fan, Chan provides what Rebecca Bell-Metereau calls an "alternative to the binary model" of straight and gay, a "third space ... non-gendered norm which blur[s] the distinctions and celebrate[s] the 'slippage' of category terms."[58] Fan Fan is a free-floating signifier (she travels the world, after all, on a yacht), has meaningful heart-to-heart conversations with males and females, enjoys sleeping with both Sam and Wing, seems to share an intimate friendship with her lesbian assistant, and yet remains a mystery to us. Her similarities with Anita Mui herself (often referred to in the west as the "Hong Kong Madonna"), and the shared absence of a childhood and presence of celebrity (Michael Jackson, alluded to in both films) blur boundaries further. Whether Fan Fan is indeed a lesbian, straight, or bisexual is never answered and ultimately, according to Chan at least, unimportant. She is the always out-there elusive possibility of otherness (recall at the music awards, the room is abuzz with anticipation that Fan Fan will appear; instead, O breezes through on roller blades to pick up her award).

Ed Sikov, in writing of 1950s American comedies, observes: "Characters of course have no psyches; audiences do. Defined by the culture from which they arise, film characters of both genders appeal to their audience's infantile bisexual core in partial defiance of the particular repressions and expressions of their age."[59] Examining gender matters and sexual orientation in both *He's a Woman* and *Who's the Woman*, one concludes, at face value, based on audience reception, that homophobia in regard to lesbianism is considered more taboo than homosexuality. Taken together, the films reframe gender issues, with the sequel more clearly challenging heteronormative understanding of sexual preference.

In another vein, Kwai-cheung Lo, in *Chinese Face/Off*, criticizes simplistic gender representation in Wing's characterization in the first film and instead argues that "[Wing's] unbound sexual identity is, in fact, more compatible with the fantasy of the global flow of capitalism than with criticism of traditional concepts of gender,"[60] providing another direction for gender appropriation in Chan's film (see Chapter 4). But there is another way of understanding the cross-dressing, sexual orientation, and gender issues that have been the focus of this chapter. In both of Chan's pre-1997 films, gender issues can be related to the looming 1997 question at the time.[61] Not only was there "high anxiety" among the Hong Kong population about their futures, despite Article 5 of Hong Kong Basic Law that post-1997, Hong Kong would become the Special Administrative

Region, operating as it had under the British as a colony. Deng Xiaoping's promise of "one country, two systems," that Hong Kong would remain the same for 50 years, was questioned in general by many typically apolitical Hong Kongers. More narrowly, among gay and straight Hong Kongers concerned with individual rights and specifically the status of the rights of sexual minorities, uncertainties loomed. (Even Leslie Cheung's "coming out" concerts of the *World Tour '97* can be understood as reflective of political "high anxiety.") Although the Law Reform Council had discussed the subject of homosexual rights in 1980, the Hong Kong Legislative Council had only decriminalized homosexuality with the Crimes (Amendment) Bill of 1991, making it official. Prior to this law, punishments ranged from two years in prison for "gross indecency" to a potential lifetime sentence for consenting adult males engaged in anal intercourse.[62] With Hong Kong making some progress in regards to gay rights, what would the result be considering the PRC's record of persecution of homosexuals (during the Cultural Revolution there were long-term prison sentences and even execution)? The Motherland's homophobia included regarding homosexuality as a mental disorder (this changed in 2001 when the new *Chinese Classification and Diagnostic Criteria of Mental Disorders* removed homosexuality from its listing, essentially starting a "don't ask, don't tell" or "out of sight, out of mind" policy regarding Mainland officials). Still, despite some progress, the PRC and many Chinese heterosexuals (including Hong Kongers) continue to view homosexuality as a social disgrace and taboo. Consider Mary Wong Shuk-han's critical commentary on gay filmmaker Stanley Kwan's *Hold You Tight* (1998) in *Contemporary Chinese Cinema: 1998*, where she lambastes the film for "the 'sacrifice' of marriage and heterosexuality for the existence of queerness and gay people."[63]

Ironically, China's history of homosexuality as an acceptable practice is well documented, dating back to the Han Dynasty emperors (202–220 BCE) as well as being exercised well into the 18th century in Fujian Province (by young men until they married); it has been memorialized in the visual arts, philosophy, opera, and literature; in scroll paintings, *hsiang-kung* (beautiful young male actors playing female parts in operas, available for hire for pleasure), Taoism; and episodes in respected literary works such as *The Water Margin, Dream of the Red Chamber*, and *Romance of the Three Kingdoms*. Although homosexual practices continued during the Qing Dynasty (1644–1900 CE), a conservative turn manifested when laws became harsher against behavior considered "deviant," such as homosexuality. The persecution that continued throughout the 20th century, under the republic and the communist regime,[64] suggests a social amnesia, and Grossman sees "the recovering of homosexuality as a lost symbol of Chinese diversity ... [as] the means to acknowledging a Chinese past within the context of H[ong] K[ong]'s democratic dilemma."[65] As recently as Summer 2006, the PRC banned the popular South Korean film *The King and the Clown* from screening in theaters (a movie that grossed US$85 million on its home turf) due to "homosexual themes and bad language."[66] Paradoxically, the Chinese government invited Leslie Cheung as a featured guest for its celebration spectacle of the return of Hong Kong to the Motherland on 1 July 1997, and Cheung's presence and performance was one of the highlights of the festivities.

Chan's humanism flavors both films. Intertwining the comedy with more serious issues, Chan avoids grandstanding; instead, the comic and dramatic functions are related through the human experience. The director has great affection for his characters but recognizes their human foibles, contradictions, and ambiguities, and the social constructs we build to live together while also acknowledging "the gap between existence as it is and as it ought to be."[67] Mast recognizes Charlie Chaplin "whose great gift was his ability to convey moral attitudes without moralizing,"[68] an attribute

Chan emulates here. The sequel would provide a culturally radical affirmation of gender difference, both disruptive and subversive, and therefore potentially opening space and power for non-mainstream gendering, sexual discovery, and transformation, more closely akin to the politically challenging independent new queer cinema that emerged in the 1990s, especially when contrasted with the homophobia that plays for comedy in many mainstream Hong Kong movies of this era and presently.

Mast concludes, "The most effective film comedies — as well as the most thought-provoking ones — are mimetic rather than didactic, descriptive rather than prescriptive. They present a picture of a particular social or human condition without tacking on a simplistic moral solution to the comic problems, and without telling the viewer to apply the solution to his own life ... . The human problems ... do not admit easy solutions."[68] In all fairness, like all good movies, Chan's pair of films raises questions rather than provides answers, and they definitely got people laughing and talking — a good thing.

4

Commerce and Globalization

"I want a man. An ordinary man, even if he doesn't look good or can't sing. It doesn't matter. Just let me recommend him and help him until he is a success, then we can prove to the world that there is still hope for them. This is the true miracle and legend of the music industry." — Sam in *He's a Woman, She's a Man*.

Hong Kong cinema of the 1980s and 1990s, rooted in the historic conjuncture of its colonial and post-colonial relations between Britain and its ties to the Mainland, can be described as "crisis cinema" as new patterns of language, time and space, place and identity, and meaning itself arose. The return of Hong Kong to the Mainland served as text and subtext for filmmakers, and after the crackdown on Tiananmen Square in 1989, Hong Kongers themselves were more politically active than perhaps at any other historical moment. According to Nick Browne, "Narratively speaking, the temporal mode of Hong Kong cinema is not retrospective, but future anterior — a syncretic culture caught in the complexity of an impending return that threatens to be a future undoing of its past achievement."[1] I do not wish to underplay the significance of crisis cinema. Chan's gender-bending surely can be read as gender crisis substituting for the political one, particularly in light of the high anxiety of gays and lesbians in anticipation of a government crackdown on non-heterosexuality, based on illiberal Mainland laws, as well as in relation to the political economy of Hong Kong and its commercialism in contrast to the then perception of a slowly changing Mainland economy. But to attempt to analyze the film as highly structured with Wing's mistaken identity and Sam's identity crisis as political allegory of colonial Hong Kong society would be limiting and forcing the narrative into something it is not. And clearly, the idea of change on the horizon and time running out provided the impetus for creativity as well as the commercial push to make money fast (as well as raised concerns among liberals regarding the rights of sexual minorities). However, other equally significant aspects, namely commerce and globalization, deserve discussion.

Despite its small size, in the 1990s Hong Kong's film industry ranked third internationally in film production (behind Hollywood and India), second (to the US) in film export, and first in the world in per capita production,[2] until the Asian economic crisis hit in October 1997 and Hong Kong experienced its fallout in 1998. Hong Kong cinema was characteristically regional (with presales across the Asian market) and international (in diasporic Chinatowns worldwide, with North and Latin American urban populations, film festivals, and across college campuses). It has, over the last 50 years, not only been commercial but has capitalized on Hollywood trends, emerging full-blown as a transnational and globalized cinema, reflecting the flow of global capital during the 1990s. Its early 1990s cinema benefited from the acme reached in the late 1980s, and suffering through the economic crisis, Hong Kong has attempted to rebound since, with some highs and lows.[3] Hong Kong's participation in co-productions on the Mainland increases annually, and its production and distribution deals, including its own product as well as the selling of film concepts, (with remakes like Martin Scorsese's *The Departed* [2006], adapted from Andrew Lau/Alan Mak's *Infernal Affairs* [*Mou gaan dou/Wu jian dao* (2002)]), claim its place in the global market. Locating *He's a Woman* historically and critically in this larger context raises several issues, one being how western (specifically Hollywood) cultural forms have been appropriated by the Hong Kong filmmaker for a home audience, another being the recent globalization of Chinese cinemas. Sheldon Hsiao-peng Lu, in his *Transnational Chinese Cinemas*, explains the need for "a new theoretical description" for Chinese cinemas, and the current vernacular in use is "Chinese language cinema," circumventing the local and national and emphasizing the international and global.[4] How do we traverse language and acknowledge the methodological constraints, including the temporal, economic, geographic, and language, placed on cultural products, factual information, and analysis? And how do we draw conclusions based on these limitations? Taking a cue from Edward Said,[5] we also want to avoid imposing a western perspective on the east, circumventing a critical imperialism by relying on Hong Kong sources and audience, and also acknowledging Peter Chan, a Hong Kong Chinese who spent his formative years in Thailand with some education in the US, and his pan-Asian and global perspective.

One consideration is, as Rey Chow argues, "film has always been, since its inception, a transcultural phenomenon, having as it does the capacity to transcend 'culture' — to create modes of fascination which are readily accessible and which engage audiences in ways independent of their linguistic and cultural specificities."[6] As a visual medium, film speaks everyone's language and is therefore open to all comers, freed from a master narrative. Multiple readings lead to interpretations contingent on their historical moment and a whole web of factors, leading to contention, recognition of otherness, and ultimately, enrichment. As sociologist Mike Featherstone, with a more positive take on globalism than some, astutely observes in *Undoing Culture: Globalization, Postmodernism and Identity*, "The globalization process should be regarded as opening up the sense that now the world is a single place with increased contact becoming unavoidable, we necessarily have greater dialogue between various nation-states, blocs and civilizations: a dialogical space in which we can expect a good deal of disagreement, clashing of perspectives and conflicts, not just working together and consensus."[7] Kwai-cheung Lo specifically locates the clash of cultures in 1990s Hong Kong cinema, and notes "the local constructed ... is an area of negotiation within which dominant, subordinate, and oppositional cultural, economic, and ideological elements are mixed in various permutations."[8] Chan's film proves an apt example.

Also to consider as a part of the global picture is film distribution and viewing. These include the media transformation resulting from the emergence of recent technologies, such as the constantly evolving Internet and the rise of innumerable film communities, as well as the invention and dissemination of video formats, including the (now dinosaur) laser disc, VCD, and DVD. More recently, the advent of movies on demand through companies such as DirecTV, and wired sources, such as NETFLIX and YouTube, has introduced new modes for film viewing, with both positive and negative results. One the one hand, the once "collective experience" of watching a movie on a big screen in a theater with a live audience, so aptly described by Walter Benjamin, is eroding.[9] Instead, film viewing becomes a selfish act, individual, private, and convenient, no longer a shared experience. Even in virtual communities online, the community is always at a distance. On the other hand, these border-crossing cultural flows are scattering and fostering international films to a global audience, expanding and developing new audiences (and customers) for film product.

He's a Woman situates its gendered subjects within a specific social context (urban, cosmopolitan, and almost post-colonial and post-return) and simultaneously within an always-already transnational, transcultural, and global space, given the nature of Hong Kong's historical, cultural, and economic development itself. The characters emerge from the world of Hong Kong pop music and fandom, with the story opening during the televised Hong Kong Music Awards. References to the local abound, from the Cantopop heavenly kings[10] to fan club rivalries (Leon Lai fans are singled out for an attack, and when Leon Lai's "Summer of Love" is performed during the audition, it is by a mime).[11] Wing complains about her peeping tom landlord and the noise from Kai Tak Airport, her cramped and shared working-class apartment adjacent to the old Kowloon-based airport. Otherwise the city itself remains anonymous, with city space utilized as generic background[12] (seen from rooftops or huge Victoria Peak picture windows, characters getting into or out of cars, gathered fans on an otherwise characterless street). Identifiable architectural landmarks are lacking (if you look closely you can see the Bank of China outside the picture window from the Peak, but it is indistinct) and the exteriors are without character. Instead, settings are dominated by interiors — the apartments of the working class and elite, the various spaces of the workplace, or the ambience of chi-chi restaurants and clubs.

Scholar Ackbar Abbas has clearly characterized Hong Kong as a transitional space where, through people's cultural experience (including film, architecture, photography, and literature), that space becomes an abstraction that undoes history and presence. He explains, "There is a need to define a sense of place through buildings and other means, at the moment when such a sense of place (fragile to begin with) is being threatened with erasure by a more and more insistently globalizing space."[13] Mutability has always been a characteristic of Hong Kong. In the 1990s, Hong

Kong had an approximate population of 6.5 million people, an average hyperdensity of 40,000 persons per square mile (Hong Kong then comprised 414 square miles on one principal island, Hong Kong; a peninsula, Kowloon; and, former hinterlands, the New Territories), and Hong Kong's skyline continually remakes itself, with postmodern commercial structures reaching 28 stories and apartment buildings 20–34 storys being the usual.[14] Constant demolition of perfectly useful older buildings makes way for the new, with reconstruction the norm. Abbas refers to "the changing cultural space of the city," and notes "the cultural self-invention of the Hong Kong subject in a cultural space of disappearance."[15] The generalization of Hong Kong and the absence of the current cityscape in Chan's film covers over a lack, reflecting both a nostalgia for a disappearing city and citing a mental cartography that overlooks attention to the material and historical conditions that created it; physical space and local geography are, for all purposes, non-existent.

There have long been border-crossing flows of capital, labor, raw materials, and goods internationally, and since its emergence as a newly industrialized city-state, Hong Kong (now the SAR, Special Administrative Region, since its return to the Motherland) serves as a way station for such flows, retaining the world's freest market economy and most service-oriented economy. David R. Meyer notes "the integration of telecommunications and computer technologies that permit instantaneous transmission of information ... rais[ing] anew the specter that key actors in finance, commodity exchange, corporate management, and other businesses controlling exchange of capital will dispense from their metropolitan bases" and cites studies from the Center for Asian Pacific Studies which identify Hong Kong as "one of the greatest concentrations of decision-makers controlling exchanges of world capital."[16] Hong Kong's economic miracle in the 1960s and soaring trade, which began in the 1970s, continues expansion, despite the Asian economic crisis, due in large part to its resilience and its networking position with foreign and Mainland Chinese capital. Peter Dicken, in *Global Shift*, distinguishes between "internationalization" and "globalization," the latter differentiated by rapid technological development, increased border trade, investment, migration, and more complex integration of dispersed activity.[17] Many economists have noted the decline of nation-state sovereignty and weakening national cultural identity (even more problematic with Hong Kongers' ties to the Mainland), also happening in Hong Kong, along with the relocation of "back-office white collar jobs" to the Mainland while corporate headquarters remain.[18] Roland Robertson prefers the term "glocalization," suggesting intensive local and global interaction.[19] Considering the local is overwhelmed in Hong Kong by multi-national and corporate brands from McDonalds and Sony to HVM and Starbucks, how can the local compete?

Surely part of a sense of one's identity is tied to localism and a sense of place — where one plants one's feet, where one considers home to be. What does it mean to be Hong Kong Chinese, and how does such a person understand her/his identity? While Mainland China has served as the homeland and motherland for most (even among Hong Kong belongers, those among the post–Cultural Revolution generation born and raised in Hong Kong are known to refer to Mainland China as motherland), as Steve Tsang, in *A Modern History of Hong Kong*, points out, "Hong Kong ... indeed acquired a sense of identity, way of life and value system in its British period that set it apart from those prevailing in Mainland China."[20] He believes that local people began reflecting on their sense of identity with the signing of the Joint Declaration in 1984, which he describes as "confused," especially in regards to their "contradictory view of Sino–Hong Kong relations."[21] He also adds that during and following the June 4th Movement (the student democratic movement in the PRC), "Most Hong Kong people's identification with the 'democracy movement' turned them, in their own minds, into the student protesters' instant comrades."[22] Rozanna Lilley emphasizes the Mainland ties in relation to Hong Kong identity but notes the "ambiguity and flux of forms of identification, the ways in which some local people could simultaneously be faithful to the notion of being Chinese, locate the center of that 'Chineseness' in the Mainland, distrust the current government of China, be proud that colonial rule was ending, feel deeply attached to Hong Kong and be cynical about the future possibilities of their lives under Chinese rule."[23] Identity is always in a state of flux, but complicated even more so for Hong Kongers. With a constantly changing local landscape to boot, both in conflict and synch with the global, sense of identity and defining the local become a fertile source for creativity. Lilley adds, "Individuals involved in local performing arts [and in this I would include filmmaking] suggest that they are self-consciously trying to create a Hong Kong identity [to escape] the double bind … of the persistence of 'tradition and contemporaneity' as narrations within a cultural polemic that refuses us solid terms like 'decolonization,' that offers up only chimerical slippages between ancient China and a slick metatopical space of global financing."[24] How Chan maneuvers between the local and global in the same space to create a sense of identity cannot be separated from the gender and sexual politics of the movie. Home can also be inside or outside a closet.

Kwai-cheung Lo also uses the term "glocalization" to describe the current "Asianization" of Hong Kong film and its strategy of "global localization." Lo explains, "Although Hong Kong appears to address its differences from others, the city is actually struggling with itself, with its place in the world, and with its own invented sense of Chineseness. The depiction of localism in Hong Kong films proves to be a circular journey in which the more globalized localism becomes, the more it is nationalized — or re-localized … . It never returns to its starting point because the so-called national or ethnic point of origin is continually differentiated."[25] Lo argues that Hong

Kong cinema's "glocalization" is more transnational than national in its ideology, so evident in Chan's film, which is set in another world, both local and international, the world of fandom. Lo notes the multiple appearances of paparazzi and crazed fans, and surmises, about Hong Kong: "The logic of commodification dominates the local popular culture: the individual style and talent of the artists simply comprise a package produced by the music industry, while the fans are not too innocent to take advantage of their idols by selling their photos of them and accessories they have used. The local culture is therefore depicted as totally capitalized and commercially exploited."[26] Several scenes in the movie dramatize this characterization, from the YES star collectibles officially being sold to the illegal hawkers displaying their wares and Wing ransacking Sam's apartment for personal items to sell. The self-referentiality of the auditions as performance and artistic self-consciousness are delightfully doubled by the presence of singing and acting star (Cheung) as a judge, with some wannabe performers covering Cheung's and other Cantopop songs. And while audition scenes have appeared in numerous films, Chan not only cites local stars but seems to anticipate the current taste du jour of US television's *American Idol*, a pre-fab "reality" contest with faux audience participation, in which there are some winners and mostly losers, but instant notoriety for all, with some of the losers gaining fame and lucrative contracts.

The notion that any male (talented or not) can become a singing star and celebrity success simply as a product fashioned by the industry is driven home by several elements in the film. First is the transformation of Michelangelo's iconic "Creation of Adam" from the *Sistine Chapel Ceiling*, now a visual billboard advertisement for the singing contest (which reads "as long as you're a man"), and with a gold-plated microphone added in God's hand, handing off to Adam, the passing of the torch, so to speak, from father to son (or, musically, producer to singer). The image introduces the audition montage and Wing's preparation for it, both set to the tune of Handel's "Entrance of the Queen" from *Solomon*. Secondly, Sam's dialogue ("This is the true miracle and legend of the music industry") in an appropriate straight-on facial close-up as the camera slowly moves in, and Cheung leans in, is followed by slow pans of parts of the "Creation" (emphasizing male anatomy) accompanied by Handel's memorable "Hallelujah Chorus" from *The Messiah*, with its resounding praise of the blessed event audiences are about to witness (the creation of a singing sensation that will effect change on the music scene, in this case, Wing's androgynous look). Hence, a commercial film capitalizes on a commercially driven industry supported by local profiteers and exploited globally.

Chan appears to have it both ways, creating a hybrid identity that quotes the local scene but translates it for the global spectator.[27] He found his cue in the Cantopop style itself and in his lead, Cantopop singer Cheung, whose public figure struck a similar chord. Leslie Cheung's singing career began with him singing Don McLean's "American Pie" in the local Asian Amateur Singing Contest (he was first runner-up), and his first release, 1977's *Daydreamin'* consisted of covers of American pop songs (all sung in English). He would also have an Elvis phase, at least in his dress and look. While this Anglophilia seemingly suggests a westernized and global perspective, Cheung freely admitted his admiration for local sensation Roman Tam, and his next release, 1979's *Lover's Arrow* (aka *Love Arrow*) is largely a Tam-style release.[28] Throughout his career, Cheung would cater to a local audience, always including older and much loved tunes, such as "Dream," made popular by Lin Dai (as sung by Carrie Koo Mei) in *Love Without End* (1961) and much sentimentalized Mainlander Teresa Teng's "The Moon Represents My Heart." In the film, as Sam, Cheung's character's first song is an enthusiastic English cover of the Beatles' "Twist and Shout,"[29] with Sam on piano jamming with his father's old cronies, and at one point Wing joins in with Sam and the boys in a reprise (with cigar and crotch scratch to hand). How do informed viewers perceive this but as a part of the Cantopop culture? There have been English language hits in Hong Kong. But the film opens with a Cantonese cover of Dean Martin's signature "That's Amore," and most of the songs Sam sings are in Cantonese and the Cantopop style, that is, the local flavor. Borders prove shifting sands in any attempt to locate a uniquely Hong Kong Chinese culture, whose very hybridity may be the only way to singularize it in the borderless contemporary world.

Chan sees himself as an urban filmmaker, explaining, "I grew up in cities all my life and I believe lives in contemporary cities are very similar wherever you are ... I'd like to be able to work in different places and make films that are basically about lives in the city." Both urbanization and capitalization (in the sense of both capitalism and profit, capitalizing on and exploiting an image) are incorporated in a visual medium to construct the various gender and global identities in the story. The womanly Rose, for example, wants to travel to Vienna, not for the music, but the shopping; the dissatisfied Sam, to the contrary, desires a safari in the abstract Africa, influenced by Paul Simon's "discovery" of world music and himself searching for inspiration. The inexperienced Wing simply wants to get close to her idols, but once there, finds ways to improve her lot. All have something missing from their lives, and, as Chan relates, "People are having the same problems, going through the same kind of crises: relationships, midlife, friendships. That has always been the theme of all my films."

The cosmopolitan Chan defines globalism as "the world getting smaller and smaller," which he also cites as a theme in all of his movies, explaining "they could play anywhere, the only difference being the language in which dialogue was spoken."[30] The humor and emotions can basically be understood by anyone, and Chan's style of shooting, storyline, and global references (primarily western) make him an international filmmaker with a sure hand.

Cultural products are both seen and heard, from Garfield, *Sesame Street*'s Ernie and the Count, HMV music stores, and the American flag to western classical music samplings (Handel, Beethoven, Bach, Boccherini, Chopin), western rap, and rock. Numerous American commodities appear, beginning with the opening tracking shot from a cockroach's point of view, amidst the wrappers and peanut shells, dominated by Coca-cola, along with Schwepps, and a Garfield slipper. Gina Marchetti has noted product placement and "the spectacle of global consumerism" in Wong Kar-wai's *Chungking Express*, in which Faye Wong's character is inside a store purchasing a huge stuffed Garfield while Brigitte Lin's is framed "in front of ... [the] shop window brimming with toys, small electrical goods, and a variety of colorfully packaged gadgets."[31] Chan's "global localization" creates a fusion culture, defining Hong Kong identity not as a site of resistance to global capital but as a source of embrace. Regarding Hong Kong cinema, Marchetti concludes, "Global products with American labels define the cultural landscape."[32] Chan's hold on global capital culture in this film, however, moves beyond the commodity to citation of western cultural references and even people themselves.

Chan admires filmmaker Woody Allen, and the director serves as the model for Sam not attending the music awards but hanging out at a music club to jam with the old-timers (just as Allen for years played clarinet at a New York club rather than attend the Academy Awards ceremonies).[33] Many western viewers call to mind Blake Edwards's *Victor/Victoria*[34] (1982) or Sydney Pollack's *Tootsie*[35] (1982) as points of reference, but besides involving cross-dressing, a heterosexual relationship thought by one of the parties to be homosexual, and figures succeeding in entertainment, the films share mostly superficial similarities. Numerous overlapping and borrowings lead Lo, in *Chinese Face/Off*, to go further in his critique, stating that the juggling, syncretizing, and simulating of "Chineseness" in Chan's films and others of the 1990s not only create an "emergent transnational imaginary," but are in fact "a new type of cultural imperialism."[36] Lo describes the transnational imaginary as "the privileged and global appropriation of peripheral, localist cultures for mainstream reimagining."[37] Chan's erasure of the local thus becomes the general global. As one viewer puts it, "People everywhere can relate to the music/movie business. People across the world are fascinated with it and wonder what it would be like to be a part of it."

The world of fandom allows a space in which fans create and recreate their identities. Wing is several times described as "an ordinary person," and it can be argued both that she is transformed through fandom into a star (wish fulfillment) and that she remains the ordinary person for whom Sam longs. Wing as "ordinary person" draws on "portraits of life in the lower depths" in comedies written by Chinese playwrights and translated to the screen in movies such as *The House of 72 Tenants*.[38] The working-class Wing and Yu Lo (Fish) mirror "the 'little guys' trying every possible means to make a living and dreaming of an abundant life"[39] that appeared in Hong Kong post–World War II comedies. Cheung Yu describes Cantonese comedy characters of the 1950s and 60s as "reflect[ing] certain thinking and attitudes of the society of their time. They expressed the dreams and the collective unconscious mind of a certain social stratum."[40] Similarly, Wing and Yu Lo (Fish) offer a contemporary version of the everyman character that can also be seen in the piglet McDull in Toe Yuen and Brian Tse's *McDull* animated series (drawing on their McMug comics) and as represented by Tony Leung Chiu-wai's Wai Siu-po in the TVB television series "The Duke of Mount Deer" (based on Jin Yong's *The Deer and the Cauldron*). Practical, stubborn, with a can-do attitude, both Wing and Yu Lo (Fish) are also kind-hearted and loyal; yet both are dreamers, Yu Lo fantasizing about numerous women, Wing about her idols. Their cramped apartment is plastered with pictures of singing and movie stars, and class differences between them and Sam and Rose are made explicit by their respective living spaces. The visual juxtapositions between characters and settings, and Wing's invasion of the office space and the couple's digs gain her entry into another social level, and with the elevator and hidden staircase linking Sam and Rose's quarters, the plotting becomes a Chinese "upstairs, downstairs," Wing and Sam a Hong Kong "odd couple," and their flat-sharing definitely urban as opposed to traditional rural morality. Wing's moving in with Sam repeats "the pattern of the dividing wall" labeled by Ng Ho, where a comical war ensues in a battle of the sexes.[41] One female spectator notes, "I found myself identifying with Wing, pretty much all the way through. From the start, she is the ordinary person that lives in the messy apartment that we are led to identify with, as opposed to the higher-profile characters of Sam and Rose. The opening shot is very … how can I put it, 'inviting'? as it tracks the viewpoint of this bug … the 'on the ground' perspective. Wing is taken from her commonness and made into a star that rises and hobnobs with the top in the Hong Kong industry."

Wing's primary visual function is cuteness (she is doubled by a little girl dressed identically in one of the opening scenes), which makes it easy and convenient for spectators to find the character's meaning rather than having to invent their own connection to a film "product." She is virtually asexual and therefore non-threatening, and she remains infantile and adolescent (at least, in the first film). Flat-chested or underdeveloped, Wing requires only a simple taping around her chest to allow her to pull off the disguise (this scene plays to comic effect, even though the womanizing Yu Lo wraps her). This physical attribute indicates an amorphous quality, because paradoxically Wing also exhibits a plainness that allows her to be filled with meanings by others, and spectators, no matter their age, can live vicariously through her as they consume the film, by projecting their own feelings onto the character; thus two people of different generations can enjoy the character for very different reasons.[42] Wing is a dreamer, whose dreams come true (and at moments, she is reminded, we should all be careful what we wish for).[43] She also signals female empowerment through the fairy tale ending. Wing's fantasy, which she has actively helped bring about, comes true. And, furthermore, the fantasy element of the film (and the sequel) plays into the wish fulfillment of film-goers who live voyeuristically and vicariously through larger-than-life characters onscreen.

The marketing of the film capitalized on the fantasy. *He's a Woman* spawned two soundtracks, one with Cheung, Anita Yuen, and Carina Lau singing on it, the other with the same songs sung by relatively unknowns, to coincide with the plotline of creating images and singing stars and the chance that there are infinite possibilities for an "ordinary person" to be discovered. "Gum sang gum sai" ("In My Life"), which became a Cheung standard in concerts, was sung by Dick Lee. There was also limited production of a special edition collector's set for the laser disc housed in a traditionally styled woman's mirror box (albeit of sturdy cardboard). It included Leslie Cheung's face reflected in its mirror (a manufactured image and returned gaze), so that as you looked into the mirror you would see not only your own image but your image superimposed upon Cheung's, and various collectibles such as lobby cards, a watch with Cheung's smiling face, playing cards, rose-themed gift cards, and an inscribed card with attached dried roses similar to the one Sam has given Rose in the movie. As in the fairy tale film ending, fantasy became reality.

Marchetti notes "The consumption of commodities promises a new identity; however, the commodity may insistently shape that identity in unexpected and underappreciated ways. As the echoes of Hollywood in Hong Kong seem to indicate, cinema plays a role in the display of people and goods transnationally."[44] *He's a Woman* puts its stars, especially Cheung, on display and for sale; they become the new commodity for a global marketplace. The British punk band The Clash effectively labeled the cult of personality phenomenon as "the right profile" (in reference to Hollywood actor Montgomery Clift[45]), but Belgian theorist Walter Benjamin was among the first to accurately describe it as "the cult of the movie star, fostered by the money of the film industry, [which] preserves not the unique aura of the person but the 'spell of the personality,' the phony spell of a commodity."[46] Not only are music stars in the film presented as commodities for sale within the story, but this representation is compounded by Hong Kong movie stars playing music stars, thus leading to the self-reflexive nature and doubling of the film's ideology. The personalities of the actors are instrumental in both creating the comedy (mostly playing against type) and in selling the film (they are advertisements for a cultural product). Indeed, the film self-referentially comments on the notion of image-making and illusion. As Rose peers in the mirror, Wing asks "But aren't you just creating an illusion?" "Such is human nature," Rose replies. Of course, the irony of the situation is that Wing is also a victim of the illusion of the story of Sam and Rose as well as creating an illusion for them, her masquerading as an androgynous gay male.

Besides his infamous statement comparing actors to cattle, Hitchcock once remarked, "Casting is characterization,"[47] and the casting of Cheung, Yuen, and Lau as the leads (and Mui in the sequel) carries great weight in the thematics of both films. The known personalities of Cheung and Mui especially were important in shaping both films. Both began as scrappers, both participated in singing competitions, becoming fast friends during their salad days. "Crossover"[48] is common from singing to screen (either television or film) and many former Miss Hong Kongs become movie stars (usually until they marry, at which time many retire).

The descriptions of these actors at Kozo's popular website "Love HK Film" illustrate their reputations. Cheung, whose nickname was "Gor Gor" (Big Brother) is called "Hong Kong's own son ... an

institution in Hong Kong (and the rest of the Chinese diaspora) ... .
He is bigger than just about anyone in Hong Kong — an enormously
popular singer for two decades and one of the bigger box-office
draws for years. People — including grandmothers along with their
teenage and preteen grandchildren — just love Leslie."[49] Cheung's
characterizations are described as "self absorbed but oh so
attractive ... intriguing [with his] perpetual pout ... [and] a flare for
the dramatic ... his outrageousness, his charm, his quick smile, his
outbursts."[50] Anita Mui is portrayed as "a huge star in both the
music and the film worlds since the mid-'80s" and Kozo notices
the similarities between her real life and the past attributed to her
character in *Who's the Woman, Who's the Man?* "Her father died
when she was young and she toured as a young girl with her
mother's cabaret group ... She often sang in lounges with her sister
Ann as well to earn money."[51] Anita Yuen, "endearing and lovable
at the same time," a former Miss Hong Kong, is personified as "the
'It Girl'" of Hong Kong film with a series of comedies that tickled
the funny bones of audiences throughout Asia. Her quirky
characters, wide-eyed gamine look, and appealing grin captured
the hearts of men and women alike. Her unique short-haired coiffed
style was a sensation and it had nearly every teenaged girl in Hong
Kong asking her local beauty parlor for the "'Anita' look."[52] And
lastly, Carina Lau's sensuality and womanliness are noted in "Love
HK Film," which states that she is "a total woman — not half
woman/half girl as so many Hong Kong actresses tend to be these
days. She is also one of the finest actresses in Hong Kong."[53]

Director Ronny Yu, who directed Cheung in both *The Bride
with White Hair/The Evil White-Haired Lady* (*Baak faat moh nui/
Bai fa mo nu*, 1993) and *Phantom Lover/Midnight Song* (*Ye boon
goh sing/Ye ban ge sheng*, 1995), aptly compared his image
onscreen to James Dean and Johnny Depp.[54] Cheung also
resembled 1950s and 60s actor Chang Yang in looks and versatility,
the older actor having played in comedies and dramas, often as

sensitive and wounded, and also Zheng Junmian, known as "the Oriental Elvis Presley ... [His] look was suggestive of teddy boys or playboys."[55] Wong Kar-wai, Patrick Tam, and Lawrence Lau cast Cheung as *ah fei* (disaffected youth) characters. With his androgynous appeal and boyish good looks, he became known for playing elusive charmers that bring people close but keep them at a distance. With a slight overbite, sensuality, grace and subtle humor, skill as singer and dancer, Cheung also had impeccable timing — as in *He's a Woman*, subtly delayed responses at crucial moments hold audiences' attention. Even as a bad boy, spectators had to love him. He was equally good in comedy, drama, and action. In comedies such as John Woo's *Once a Thief (Criss Cross Over Four Seas)/Jung waang sei hoi/Zong heng si hai* (1991), Raymond Wong's *All's Well Ends Well (Family Has Happy Affairs)/Ga yau bei si/Jia you xi shi* (1992) and *It's a Wonderful Life (Big Rich Family)/Daai foo ji ga/Da fu zhi jia* (1994), Tsui Hark's *The Chinese Feast (Gold Jade Full Hall)/Gam yuk moon tong/Jin yu man tang* (1995), and Wong's *Ninth Happiness/Gau sing biu hei/Jiu xing bao xi* (1998), his insouciance carries the day, and is evident in *He's a Woman* as well. Cheung's transformation from singer to actor began with some memorable television work and some forgettable teen movies. But John Woo's *A Better Tomorrow* (*Ying hung boon sik/Yingxiong bense* [1986]) served as his serious actor calling card and Woo was impressed and concerned by Cheung's intensity when his anguished character Kit smashes his fist into a mirror; Cheung had badly cut his hand but finished the scene before being taken, at Woo's insistence, to the hospital. The film was a literal "smash" and started the "heroic bloodshed" genre. Cheung himself spoke highly of Woo and described the film as one of the most important of his career,[56] but acknowledged that his big success, recognition-wise, came with Tsui Hark/Ching Siu-tung's *A Chinese Ghost Story* (*Sin nui yau wan/Qiannu youhun*, 1988).[57] The actor made over 50 films.

A work ethic was important to him, as a singer and an actor, and Cheung told Boston film reviewer Betsy Sherman, "That's the attitude of the Chinese crowd. Even if you're sick, or maybe seriously ill, if you've not died, you still have to work."[58] Filmmakers in Hong Kong regarded Cheung the actor as a hard worker and without a big ego, and even to those who collaborated with him often, his death was a shock. Ronny Yu relates, "I was so shocked about what happened to him. Because he didn't come across as a person who's so moody. He was always the guy who came across as so charming, happy, a very positive outlook on life. And every time we were shooting, whenever I was frustrated, he would always come over and say, 'Ronny, don't worry about it. It's just a movie. The problem will solve itself.' Or, 'is there anything I can do to help you?' He helped a lot. Sometimes, when I wanted him to do those martial arts moves, it was very difficult for him, because, you know, he's not a fighter. But he was always willing to try. And he'd try and try and try. He cut his hands, he cut his feet, but he never complained. He just kept on going. Also, if the other actors and actresses complained, he'd set them straight. He'd just tell them, 'This is work. You've got to be respectful of your work. Stop complaining.' So, in a way, he was a good comrade."[59] Cheung himself confided his diffidence to June Lam, in an interview for *City Entertainment*, "Actually, I am afraid of meeting people. I hate for people to think I am stuck-up ... . Some people say I am arrogant. They don't know me, how can they say that? They can ask my colleagues, they never say that ... Facing a crew of 30 people, I feel more relaxed."[60] While the comments appear contradictory, they highlight Cheung's awareness of the image he projected and the difference between reel and real life, a part of real life for Cheung being work.

Cheung's portrayal of Sam in *He's a Woman* is not unlike his characterization of Yuddy in Wong's *Days of Being Wild/Ah Fei ching cheun/Ah Fei zheungzhuan* (1990), in some respects,[61] minus the angst and plus the comedy, a young man spoiled and vain and living in an ethereal bubble he himself finally bursts. But in addition this story includes an unmasking of Cheung, and an acting-out is indeed performed.[62] (See also Cheung's "coming-out" in Chapter 3). There is a heritage to this type of performance. Siu-leung Li quotes Cui Linqin's record of the theatrical acts of *Daimian* [The Mask] and *Damian* [The Big Face], the origins of Chinese drama in his study *Jiaofang ji* [*An Account of the Music Academy*], citing an incident set to music and songs in which a prince, Lan Ling, "was brave and heroic yet born with a face that looked like a woman's."[63] He makes a wooden mask to appear fierce on the battlefield. Li cites the mismatch between inside and outside in this historically based story as "an act of theatricality to rectify the dislocation of gender ... . To align all his inner and outer masculine gender attributes, Prince Lan Ling has to wear a mask to *perform* his masculinity ... a double-theatricalization moving in two directions: it was the performance of a performance of gender and self-referential theatrical act of acting as *masking* ... the disguise of identity. In retrospect, this very early theatrical act in Chinese cultural history subtly points to the theatricality of life itself."[64] In *He's a Woman*, Cheung's persona functions like a Beijing Opera "painted face," a mask of sorts — the supposedly homophobic and womanizing Sam (we learn Rose is his latest conquest and creation — a Sam-made female singing star) covers up someone of ambiguous sexual orientation and confused gender identity. In discussing Beijing Opera and Chen Kaige's *Farewell My Concubine/ Ba wang bie ji* (1993) and Cheung's portrayal of Cheng Dieyi, a male opera singer specializing in female roles, the actor notes, "In this movie, I am a boy; when I make up, I am an actor playing the role of a pretty young woman. And the makeup in Beijing Opera is totally white, which can cover many things."[65] So the persona conceals, but once the painted mask comes off, it falls away to reveal his feminized self at story's end (in terms of gender identity, the compassionate, cooperative, and softer side of himself; despite biological differences, males and females share both masculine and feminine qualities). And because the sexually ambiguous Cheung never officially "came out," the theatricality of his performance as a celebrity in real life, combined with the creation of celebrity as a theme of the movie, results in some jarring reverberations. Cheung may have expressed his own feelings in a song he recorded and performed "Side Face (Jak Min)," about having two faces, the public and private.[66]

While masking and unmasking is a Chinese theatrical convention, I would draw on one more metaphor to describe the image for sale of Cheung in this film, and that is the artistic technique of anamorphosis, which presents a distorted image that, when viewed at an angle or with a curved mirror, appears in its natural form. Perhaps one of the best known paintings using this practice is in Hans Holbein the Younger's (1497/8–1543) oil painting *The Ambassadors* (Jean de Dinteville and Georges de Selve) (1533), a full-length double portraiture in which French Ambassador to England Jean de Dinterville and Bishop of Lavaur Georges de Selve stand, with a table between them holding numerous accoutrements symbolizing the achievements of Renaissance learning. One image at the floor, however, is distorted, appearing as a pattern on the floor. With a curved mirror, the spectator sees a skull revealed, a *memento mori*, and the painting is generally interpreted as meaning, for all one's achievements in life, death waits for us all.[67] Considering the youthful Cheung's untimely death, and Chan's approach to the local, I find this skull, there but unseen unassisted, as an apt metaphor for both the actor's unmasking and Chan's local globalization.

Chan's exploration of the commodification of everything, including people, both describes and challenges Lo's conception of glocalization. Leslie Cheung had become, by the mid-1990s, a human commodity. The closest the greatly loved Cheung came to coming out[68] was during his "World Tour '97" concert series (promoting his new release "Red") at the Hong Kong Coliseum, which ran from 21 December 1996 through 4 January 1997. At the final concert, during encores of Teresa Teng's "The Moon Represents My Heart" and the song most associated with *He's a Woman, She's a Man,* "Chase," Cheung not only rang in the New Year, but he acknowledged his indebtedness to his longtime partner, banker Daffy Tang Hok-tak, as a family friend and his mother's godson, at the same time recognizing his mother.[69] Although everybody pretty much thought they knew Cheung's sexual orientation (gay, according to most Hong Kongers, bisexual according to some), this event comes as close as any public recognition on the actor's part to belonging to a sexual minority; even so, he was still considered to be "special." His sexual preference was euphemistically dismissed as idiosyncrasy, and he was "sold" in a variety of ways, until his demise. Cheung had his share of gay fans, and for this audience he is a visible sign of gay pride. But his fan base primarily, from the beginning, was female. We can only surmise that his lasting relationships with other female actors, including Anita Mui and Teresa Mo, were close friendships. The line blurs between Cheung's love life and the so-called romances promoted by the celebrity publicity machine and spread as tabloid fodder. Cheung reportedly confessed he was bisexual, and supposedly in his early years came close to marrying Teresa Mo (now married to director Tony Au).[70] For Hong Kongers as well as other fans, especially Asian, "it's Leslie," was their way of dealing with the image he projected and its confusing sexual politics that sadly and ultimately ignored the price of a human life with Cheung's suicide on 1 April, April Fool's Day, 2003. Some joke.[71] To this day, fan clubs and websites dedicated to Leslie Cheung and his memory remain, "selling" a variety of products, including the star. Now a legend, Cheung's words to interviewer June Lam prove haunting:

Lam: Do you feel yourself to be a Hong Kong legend?

Cheung: I can't answer that question. Whether you are or are not a legend should be answered by someone else saying it and not yourself.

Lam: Then, in your opinion, when does someone become a legend?

Cheung: After you are dead then you are a legend.[72]

After the fact, fans and industry players alike learned of Cheung's 20-year struggle with depression.[73] Although Chan's film was released in 1994, in retrospect for film spectators, the double entendres, in-jokes, and playing against typecasting now deepen the examination of the business of image-making, profits, and the machinery that keeps it all going. The pressure of maintaining "the right profile" is certainly one of the factors contributing to Cheung's suicide besides others bandied about — including his "unhappy" childhood (his description), the closet, and/or aging.[74] Peter Chan, of course, in making the film, had no idea of what was to come. But the running commentary on celebrity manufacture and its costs chillingly relates to the real world. You cannot get more local than the personal cost of a life in a hometown. Even so, only a dozen years earlier, Hong Kong had attempted to legislate social change regarding the rights of sexual minorities, catalyzed by the impending return of Hong Kong to the Mainland.

With the Crimes (Amendment) Bill, the Hong Kong government decriminalized homosexuality in 1991, in a vote of 31 to 13, yet homosexuality remains an overwhelming taboo in Hong Kong Chinese society generally.[75] In 1992, the first gay pride parade was canceled due to lack of interest,[76] and the first pink parade was held only a few years ago in 2004. A gay scene[77] has emerged slowly, but can be located and is growing more vocal and visible. Certainly, the more-than-ten-year lapse between the selection of a committee to undertake the study of a decriminalization bill and its enactment raises the ugly head of homophobia; on the other hand, the raging public and legislative discussion prior to its passage cracked open the door for more discussion, reflection regarding gender and sexual politics and identity, and affirmations by sexual minorities. Also, part of the problem of nurturing queer communities in Hong Kong is certainly due to two factors, the first being the narrowness of the Crimes (Amendment) Bill. Secondly, the enactment of the Basic Law (adopted by the Seventh National People's Congress on the Mainland on 4 April 1990), established according to the Joint Declaration between the Mainland Chinese and the British (signed on 19 December 1984, stipulating Hong Kong would remain unchanged for 50 years), did not address freedom of sexual preference, protection from hate crimes, or discrimination of sexual minorities [this is what the Crimes (Amendment) Bill tried to address].[78] In relation to film, the Hong Kong Gay and Lesbian Film Festival is representative of "the queer scene," and print criticism addressing onscreen gender construction and sexual orientation continues to grow. Filmmakers like Yonfan, Stanley Kwan, Evans Chan, and others, such as writer/theater director and choreographer Edward Lam, personify those responsible for creating an overtly gay Hong Kong cinema in recent years, although even among queer spectatorship there is debate over the queerness of the films and even defining what makes a queer film. Travis S. K. Kong, in an essay included in *Masculinities and Hong Kong Cinema*,[79] observes, first, the dual and contradictory nature of the cinema's depiction of homosexuality — while certainly heterosexual norms and hegemonic masculinity dominate, a subversive trend of homophilia has also emerged (not to mention the homophobic elements that remain in much mainstreaming cinema). Second, he notes the operation of Fredric Jameson's cultural logic of late capitalism, where Jameson sadly acknowledges that areas of our lives heretofore uncommodified have become commodified[80] — even gayness, as demonstrated in Chan's pair of films.

Chan's comic slice-of-mind provides entertainment and a source for laughter, while the dramatic elements evoke sympathy and even empathy. He achieves something more than just funny or sad, but thought-provoking, representing and dissecting the matrix of globalization and exposing the assumptions of conventional gender identity and sexual orientation, but always through character and on a directly human level. Chan makes people laugh, feel, and think at the same time. Simultaneously, Chan himself, like the Hong Kong film industry generally, is inherently commercial, and in this pair of films he sells and comments upon the selling of gayness chic. He freely admits, "I have been a very commercial filmmaker. I do care about what the marketing is. I started as a producer. You care about the investment and you have to recoup. You need to be responsible to the investors." Of the first film he admits, "I thought it was a safe movie in terms of how the audience would see it ... because we all know she's a woman." And Chan is riding the global wave. His recent film, the musical *Perhaps Love/Yu guo aoi/Ruoguo ai* (2005), produced with partner Andre Morgan, was a co-production between his Applause Pictures (a collective of filmmakers dedicated to a Pan-Asian approach, to strengthening ties between Asian-Pacific filmmakers and the industry, and to expand distribution for regional and global Pan-Asian filmmakers) and the state-owned conglomerate China Film Group on the Mainland. The follow-up, also produced by Chan and Morgan, a $40 million period piece released December 2007, was *The Warlords/Tau ming chong* (a retelling of Chang Cheh's *The Blood Brothers/Chi ma/Ci ma*, 1973).[81] Shot in Northern China, and starring Hong Kong actors Andy Lau, Kaneshiro Takeshi, and Jet Li, the film was financed by Media Asia Films, Morgan & Chan Films (Hong Kong), and China Film Group (China). Post-production took place in Hong Kong and Bangkok, and worldwide sales with numerous distributors took place at the Cannes Film Festival. Chan has just joined with Huang Jianxin of Our Production

Company and Yu Dong of Polybona to set up "Ren ren dianying gong si" ("Everybody's Movie Company"). According to Chan, they plan to shoot 15 films within three years, including over 100 million RMB blockbusters, as well as other numerous dramas. The first film will be *Dark October* (literally "October Besieged City"), directed by Hong Konger Teddy Chen (Chen Deshen).[82] Diverse aspects of film co-productions like Chan's are exploiting new technologies and transforming cultural forms. They are forging a new and ambiguous space, where distance, language, and custom continue to evolve. Is globalism the contemporary crisis or can it be a new watershed in the way we relate to each other as human beings?

5

Audience

"Hey, Big Boobs Lin, why snatch our spot? Don't you know who rules here?" — Wing to "Big Boobs Lin" in *He's a Woman, She's a Man*.

Like many other film lovers, I grew up going to the movies with adult family members, seeing the films they wanted to see, films that were beyond me at the time, such as Robert Wise's *I Want to Live!* (1958), starring Susan Hayward, and John Huston's *The Misfits* (1961), with Clark Gable, Marilyn Monroe, and Montgomery Clift. And I remember the heady days being parked with an older relative at the Saturday all-day kiddie matinee, where children ruled the theater and we were thrilled by creature features, mad scientists, insane comedies, and Sidney Furie's *The Snake Woman* (1961). Those were impressionable times, as were the late 1960s and early 1970s for my generation, with the resurgence of American cinema. My grandmother told my mother I was going to hell when I convinced her, since I was too young to be admitted, to take me to

Arthur Schlesinger's *Midnight Cowboy* (1969), but I managed to slip into the first matinee showing in my town of Dennis Hopper's *Easy Rider* (1969), although my best friend was carded and denied later that evening. Like many others, for me, college film courses and film festivals opened my world to international cinema, because where I came from, the closest we got to seeing international cinema was usually British and internationally cast and themed film, like David Lean's *Doctor Zhivago* (1965). I thanked my lucky stars when I cajoled my mother into taking a group of my friends and me to Claude Lelouch's *A Man and a Woman* (1966). She was unnerved at the (now tame) sensual and bittersweet sex scenes, but probably more appalled that it was playing at the local porno theater. Beginning in the 1980s, however, I noticed my interest waning in Hollywood product, and by that time my hometown had its own established art house and independent cinema.

My interest in Hong Kong films among international cinemas began as I turned away from overproduced, formulaic, audience-tested Hollywood product and away from over-intellectualized, international, and hip independent cinema to discover a cinema of heart and joy. Peter Chan's films deliver a sense of humor and irony in urban "dramedies." His movies bring back the pleasures of that Saturday matinee, whether it is Anita Yuen posing on the beds of Rose and Sam or Leslie Cheung smiling or puzzledly frowning into the camera. Everyone can now share in (courtesy of DVD or youtube) what was previously otherwise pirated, passed around, or discovered in the United States in Chinatowns and the now sadly disappeared Chinatown theaters.

American independent filmmaker Richard Linklater probably says it better, striking both a personal and universal chord: "I always felt cinema was a parallel life that I preferred to the real world. It probably goes back to something as childlike as sitting in a movie theatre and forgetting yourself completely as you watch this dream on the big screen. Obviously that's why film has always been so successful. It's a physical manifestation of what we all do every night, which is dream."[1] Similarly, Hong Kong director Ronny Yu, who suffered from polio as a child and was the only male in a family of sisters, evocatively recalls, "When I was a kid, I had nobody to play with, no buddies to roll around and get dirty with. I had to create my own world, my own fantasies. I lived in my own little stories."[2] He relates how his father would take him to the movies, leave the child while he worked, return for their lunch, and take him back to the theater until he completed his workday. When Yu became a filmmaker, he remembered Hong Kong director and comedian Michael Hui telling him, "Ronny, don't forget, when we die, our movies don't die. Your grandson, your great-grandson, will be watching that. Movies are immortal." Movies appeal to us by satisfying a need and, unlike people, are always available.

Linklater continues describing the cinematic experience. "It's still in you in a similar way a personal memory would be. Some of your most intense emotions or experiences come through secondary sources. For me, it was intense moments watching movies. Not that my life is devoid of intense moments, I have plenty of them, but some of the most profound, because they're so perfectly clean, because you're not directly involved, are in films. When it's your own life, you have so much baggage attached. But there's something clean about a moment in cinema that you're purely moved by."[3] Alternatively, prolific Hong Kong director and producer Tsui Hark claims, "People live in small places within themselves, and they need a place to escape, and lots of stuff in ... films offers them the opportunity to escape ... Emotion is the most essential element in my films ... mostly they're full of hope ... one always needs hope."[4] Psychoanalytic and reader-response theorist Norman Holland[5] concurs, but from the perspective of the film critic. (In the 1960s, Holland served as film critic for the *Hudson Review*). "All movies," he observes, "take us back to childhood. They give us a child's pleasure in looking at things, which we, as film critics, respond to in our demand that the film be true to its medium, that it be visual."[6] So, how do we look and why, and as critics, how do we decode what we see, as film critics focus on the added dimension of the pleasure of decoding or interpreting.

Film audience analysis can be traced back to early studies in the US and the UK at the turn of the 20th century when early movies were considered a social problem lowering moral standards in viewers. In the 1920s and 30s in the US, skewed studies concluded that movies had detrimental effects, especially on young people. Alternately, an early German study conducted by Emile Altenloh concluded that film created a public space that spoke directly to its audience.[7] Sociological studies were done in the UK in the 1930s and 40s. With the rise of the French auteur theorists in the 1950s (film critics from *Cahiers du Cinema*–turned filmmakers), film studies turned to aesthetics and film as texts to be analyzed in a vacuum, leaving their audiences behind. However, audience reception theory returned in the 1970s, with psychoanalytic theorists like Christian Metz, who came to understand audiences as spectatorial constructs and attempted to explain our pleasures and identifications with various aspects of film as a deep-seated "return of the repressed."[8] Reception theorists generally agree that "texts" (filmic or literary) are meant to be interpreted, that interpretations and the significance of "texts" are tied to their historical and cultural moment, and that interpretations change over time. Most all who write about the medium acknowledge the power of films to move us. In this holistic and empirical study we will attempt to draw conclusions based on the interactions of various audiences with *He's a Woman*, considering the contemporary social and technological processes at work as audiences watch and talk back.[9] This study draws from a written response pool of approximately 300 respondents over many years, in a variety of venues, as well as college film class viewings and discussions over the past ten years.

Film remains, since its inception, a collaborative art, not only in the way it is made, but still, to a degree, in the way in which it is experienced. Rebecca Bell-Metereau, in her Preface to *Hollywood Androgyny*, describes film as "a dynamic, negotiated 'reality' created by [the] individual viewer and culture as well as by the filmmaker."[10] Theorist Walter Benjamin, in "The Work of Art in the Age of Mechanical Reproduction," points out that "mechanical reproduction [photography] of art changes the reaction of the masses towards art" and described audience reaction to film as "progressive."[11] He goes on to marvel that audiences can appreciate and be entertained by movies and simultaneously analyze and criticize what they are watching, without pausing and contemplating, as one would a painting, but moving along with the moving images. To this approach we should add Laura Mulvey's groundbreaking study of the "male gaze," which I would take the liberty to expand to include "the heterosexual gaze" that has predominated mainstream product across the world since the invention of the art form. The so-called intended spectator's gaze established in *He's a Woman* is no different, with the movie being directed at straight audiences; however, the audience surveyed for this study includes spectators of all persuasions (as Jacques Derrida succinctly put it, "I'm for all marriages.").[12]

Benjamin furthermore characterizes film viewing as a "collective experience,"[13] i.e., social, but today such an effect is becoming either anachronistic or is at a crossroads. With the advent of video, laser disc, and DVD-viewing, and the addition of movies on demand and services such as NETFLIX and youtube, watching movies becomes a selfish act. We can do it in the privacy of our homes, at our convenience ...[14] Indie American filmmaker Kevin Smith observes: "A filmmaker's fortune isn't just dependent on ticket sales but on video-on-demand, online downloads, DVDs, and then special edition DVDs; in short, on the ardor of his devotees."[15] Smith's point emphasizes the connection between art and commerce; after all, movies are a popular culture commercial form, but he also begs the question of what is being lost, a directly shared human experience with other human beings. Consider the difference in an experience between watching a movie sitting in a theater sparsely populated or with a full house as contrasted with watching in the privacy of your home, alone, on a state-of-the-art system. Or with the convenience of a download online, watching on a laptop. Or on an airplane traveling across country, with some flyers choosing to watch and others not. What influence on our film-going experience does the environment play, especially with advancing technology? Despite the potential of technology helping us to evolve, direct presence still means something. It is tangible, and no technology has yet to reproduce the concrete feeling of it. Laughter can be infectious. As can tears. James Harvey notes, "When you're watching a comedy ... the sound of the audience around you can be almost as important as the sounds on the film."[16]

There is no accounting for taste (or arguing about it, we all have our guilty pleasures!), but what audiences accept or reject and why can help us better understand cultures and societies and what is happening at a particular historical moment. Audience analysis is one facet of film study and I believe it is worthwhile in countering narrower *l'art pour l'art* analyses. Film remains a popular art form and does not exist in a vacuum. While we probably cannot bring back the socialization of the old days with the classic large movie houses of old, with the red carpets, balustrades, and souvenir programs, or the Saturday kids' matinees where children ruled and ticket contests resulted in bike giveaways, or theme nights out at the drive-in for $1.00 a carload (Bruce Lee, Clint Eastwood, and horror flicks were the films de rigueur), what with the advance technologies of home theater systems, NETFLIX, video piracy, online downloads, etc., there is still a film-watching community, as well as Internet blogs and websites that create evolving communal film-going experiences, these latter being the latest incarnations of technological development. Film, after all, was already at one remove, in its first stages questioned as an art form because it depended on artificially seeing, assisted by a camera and technologically created. And we have adjusted to relating at a distance, seeing what the camera shows us, with (ideally) larger than life images onscreen. So I think we need to remain positive regarding film-watching and film communities. After all, with the development of the Internet, we did not stop reading, just as with the rise of the printing press and literacy, we did not stop talking. We use technology, and hopefully we exploit it (in the best sense of the word). Furthermore, a filmmaker does not work in a vacuum but creates with an audience in mind. As do actors. Leslie Cheung explained, "I only need audiences to feel my heart and sincerity."[17] So another aspect of audience is what an audience gives back. Émigré Hollywood director Billy Wilder once remarked, "Everyone in the audience is an idiot, but taken together they're a genius."[18]

So, our film community, that audience of spectators, whether packed into a theater, or seated in a sparsely populated one, or in a classroom setting with projection, or watching home alone, or online, are all being considered, including the part that the newer technologies allow. To first define our community, Stanley Fish's notion of "interpretive communities,"[19] introduced in his groundbreaking article on the two-volume Milton *Variorum* in the mid-1970s, is useful in understanding the various audiences and their reactions to the film. Fish basically transferred responsibility for the realm of possibility of interpretation from the world of the text to the reader, based on the cultural assumptions of readers (those sharing assumptions became members of the same community). Activities of readers, Fish claims, include "the making and revising of assumptions, the rendering and regretting of judgments, the coming to and abandoning of conclusions, the giving and withdrawing of approval, the specifying of causes, the asking of questions, the supplying of answers, the solving of puzzles."[20]

Fish also acknowledges the shifting sands of community membership, when he queries whether we know if we are members of the same community; his answer is "the only 'proof' of membership is fellowship, the nod of recognition from someone in the same community, someone who says to you what neither of us could ever prove to a third party: 'we know.'"[21]

We will focus on several key areas, including what most moved viewers, with whom audiences identified or felt sympathy or empathy towards, and their response to gender elements, especially regarding homosexuality, homophobia, sexual orientation and ambiguity, and gay stereotyping. We will attempt to explain why viewers have responded as they have. We will also compare audiences (Hong Kongers and Asians versus Westerners, heterosexual and queer) and their responses in these areas as compared and contrasted with Chan's stated expectations regarding reception and his intended audience.

Chan himself expected audiences to identify with Rose, and in his mind, Wing becomes the character who goes through the same thing Rose had previously — pursued by Sam, transformed by Sam, and neglected by Sam. Chan describes Wing as an "innocent girl who has all these dreams about true love and what Rose and Sam stand for in the papers, almost like Charles and Princess Di 20 years ago. She was crushed, and now she has to go through the same thing that Rose went through which is a process of her gradual loss of innocence." Wing, therefore, is the "rosebud" nurtured in the first film, both flowering and untended in the second. That most audiences did not identify with Rose caught Chan off guard. He continues, "I was quite surprised. Sam is this really selfish and pompous jerk. That really was the core of the film, and how these women became his victims. Not that he's a villain or anything, but because of his selfishness. Most of the audience did not buy Sam as a bad guy. They think he's just a regular guy, and guys are like that. Especially the women. I cannot understand that. They actually think that [Wing] is demanding, messing [up] his life. When I saw the movie with an audience, I went, 'Oh, my God!' I mean, the whole movie is structured upside down, that's what people think. But that's not what I think, I totally think Sam's an asshole. Of course I have to redeem him in the end. He's the lead."[22]

Surveying our film community in this study, audience members identified with or found sympathy or empathy for Sam, Rose, or Wing, but the majority sided with Sam. Some representative responses follow:

A 20-something male Hong Konger observes, "Sam is the person I sympathize with throughout the entire film. Although at times I do feel sad for Rose. But Sam is the person I think is the most easy [*sic*, easiest] to feel for. After all, it's Leslie." Another Hong Kong viewer explains the success of the film as due to Leslie Cheung. "The first film was very well accepted at that time mainly owing to Leslie's comeback as a singer. He announced [his singing] retirement in the late '80s and the two songs in *He's a Woman, She's a Man* became instant hits, since he hadn't released a single one for some years. The song in the sequel, 'Yau Sum Yan' ('Person with Heart,' 'Man of Intention'), was also a popular tune. Those songs remain Leslie fans' karaoke favorites." A 20-something female explains, "I sympathized with Sam's character throughout. All he wants is to find a deeper connection, a truer love, and a relationship more fulfilling than the one he has with Rose." A 20-something Latino pointed out the many pressures Sam endures: "I have sympathy with Sam Koo because he seems to always be under pressure whether by Rose or by his colleagues to sign the next greatest star out of someone ordinary. He seems to have no space for himself either. The night he comes home to the whole party, then with Rose always on his case and then with trying to make Wing a new star. He has no time for himself. It is consistent throughout the movie until the very end when he finally realizes he loves Wing whether she be a man or woman." A 35–45 year old non–Hong Kong female, for example, writes "I empathized the least with Rose and only [did so] during the last 15 minutes when I saw her grow as a person and finally take control of her own life and destiny. I connected with Sam in the sense of his being very mature, really thinking things out, and asking what's right for me and for others." Similarly, a 20-year-old non–Hong Kong male finds Sam sympathetic because of "the stress of finding new talent [and] having a selfish girlfriend" as well as puzzling over his sexual orientation. And another female viewer adds, "Sam is the most sympathetic character because he is struggling with this identity crisis of being gay or straight."

Asian audiences (Hong Kongers, South Koreans, and Japanese, natives or Americans) were familiar, for the most part, with Leslie Cheung, whereas many of the western (including Anglos, African-Americans, and Latinos) viewers surveyed mostly were not (a few had seen *Farewell My Concubine/Ba wang bie ji*). The former more easily recognized Leslie Cheung as lead and were more liable to identify or empathize with his character. Cheung's charm should be credited, as most females, including Asians and non-Asians, were willing to understand Sam's selfishness and mistreatment of Rose as the way men treat women, while they were unforgiving of Rose's need for attention.

Other females also responded to Sam, but were threatened by the gay theme. A Japanese female in her 20s suggests Sam's importance is not that he evokes sympathy, but that his situation (mistaking Wing for a gay male) is the source of most of the humor of the film, but she exhibits undertones of homophobia herself. "Sam denies his feelings of attraction to Wing because he thinks she is a man. However, because audiences already know she is a woman, his attitude makes viewers laugh. When he decides to accept the way he (or she) is, viewers are so happy to see the happy ending. Because audiences know none of them are homosexual, the story is acceptable." And another female, also in her 20s, reveals the same prejudice: "I sympathized with Sam and Wing, however, towards the end of the film my sympathy was focused on Sam. He is in love with a 'man.' It's heart wrenching to be a 'straight' man and find yourself falling in love with a man. Difficult for me to deal with." On the other hand, a gay 26-year-old Hong Konger explains, "I don't really empathize with him [Sam], but I find him pathetic not knowing what he WANTS, namely not only his sexual orientation but any ultimate goal in his life as a celebrity. It seems that his sexuality is vague." Sexuality seemed a hot button for homophobes (too much) and the queer community (not enough).

Internet responses from a variety of sources rang a similar note generally regarding Sam, emphasizing Cheung's participation. The online "Love and Bullets DVD" review, for example, describes the film as "an endearing comedy about a famous producer ... A good comedy that translates well."[23] Leslie Cheung's character is therefore most identified with in this reviewer's mind. "A Better Tomorrow Hong Kong Movies Coming Soon to DVD" remarks "the first third of the film is a bit unevenly paced as the mechanics of the plot are set in motion in (mostly) routine ways by the script. Thereafter the story takes off and the performances draw the viewer in tightly."[24] Interestingly, this source also identifies Sam Koo as the story's most important character. Sydneyguy at the "Hong Kong Movie Database" confesses "Leslie Cheung's character was the only thing that kept me barely interested"; Stardust proclaims "There is only one Hong Kong movie to date that I would be willing to say is perfect, and this is the one. Perfect and original"; jfierro remarks "Very entertaining with great performances by Anita Yuen and Leslie Cheung"; hkcinema, with three respondents, notes separately: first, "very original and entertaining plot with *excellent* music by Leslie Cheung, et al."; secondly, the plot manages "to be humorous and serious at the same time"; and, thirdly, "the situation proves to be a little preposterous, but no more so than the Elizabethan role-reversal comedies of yore."[25] These virtual audiences either focused on Cheung himself, or identified his character as the most prevalent in guiding the story.

Some viewers, all female and non–Hong Kong Chinese, sympathized with Rose, as Chan intended. To wit: A 20-year-old female writes, "The character that I became more and more attached to during the film was Rose. She was kind of preoccupied with superficial needs which was a turn off in the beginning. But what I really like about her was when Wing said something like 'Will you be my friend if I am gay?' and she replied, 'No, but I will treat you like a sister.' She was the most caring and sympathetic character in the film. Wing was annoying at first, but then playfully young and naïve. I thought Sam was horrible. Rose was so sympathetic and caring (the singing flower note) and he kind of took advantage of her." A 21-year-old, like the previous spectator, prefers Rose and blames Sam: "I sympathize with Rose because it doesn't seem like Sam really loves her, it seems like he's just using her to make money and gain publicity." Another 30-year-old adds, "My sympathies lie with Rose because she had the hardest situation to deal with. Wing was young and not as attached as Rose who was a grown-up living in a fantasy world."

On the other hand, a 21-year-old male viewer is characteristic of male reactions to Rose, calling her "the bitchy girlfriend. I empathize with Sam." Similarly, another 21-year-old male writes "In the beginning of the movie I started sympathizing with Wing. She comes across as innocent, pure, and adorable. Moreover her childish demeanor is simply loveable. This is an obvious contrast to Sam and Rose. As the movie progresses I start to feel for Sam because he begins to earnestly confront inner fears and questions about his sexuality, instead of running away from them. I in no way sympathized with or liked Rose at any point in the movie. I felt that she is desperate for male attention and bases her self-worth on male attention." These types of responses suggest an inherent sexism on the part of male spectatorship in this regard. Note that this last respondent approves of Wing's malleability.

Other males responded to Wing as well, finding her sympathetic and genuine. A 29-year-old male writes, "The most sympathetic character is Wing. I think everyone has been in a situation when we have an infatuation with someone, but just can't work up the 'balls' to be honest about our feelings. The strangest thing about this movie is the characters' willingness to live out frustrating situations. Sam and Rose continue the façade of their love life despite the strain. Wing continues the disguise of being a man despite her love for Sam. The characters refuse to take the easy way out. Sam breaks up with Rose and Wing admits she's a woman. This makes it more true to life." A 20-year-old bisexual male admits, "Wing can be quite annoying at times," but adds, "there is a certain sweetness and truth to her character that inspires sympathy. She is simply an everyday person caught in her own role, and even when in a new role, she becomes trapped as well." One more cynical 19-year-old male criticizes, "Even the little girl seems more mature than Wing."

Some viewers found no single character outstanding in regards to earning their sympathy, empathy, or identification. A 22-year-old male says, "I feel bad for everyone. They all keep lying to each other. Everyone is misled so no one knows what's going on," and another, in his early 20s, adds, "I sympathize mostly with the couple [Sam and Rose] as they go back and forth understanding that one will never understand the other."

Female audiences also differed from their male counterparts by shifting their allegiances as the story progressed. For example, one 25-year-old female explains, "At the start, [I identified with] the male character [Sam]. He had more of an average person feel, even though he had money. He still played in local clubs and it seemed as though Rose was hard on him. Towards the end, though, it was Rose. You feel that she really got hurt and all she really wanted was approval and attention. Surrounded by all those people, she still felt alone. But I really felt the most sympathy for the young girl [Wing] who was in the middle of it. She was the only one who knew the truth and she loved both of them and felt guilty for breaking them up."

Sam's developing character from supposed homophobe to indifference to sexual preference understands love. Audiences found it easy to accept this message of love, because it briefly ends the film and it was easy medicine to go down, sugarcoated, if you will, because of the fairy tale ending and because the relationships onscreen were non-threatening to traditional heterosexual values. One viewer describes Chan's message as, "When all is said and done, love conquers all." Another took the fairy tale aspect to heart: "If you dream about something long enough, it will come true." Audiences, starting with the local audience upon the film's debut, were well aware that the real actors made a straight couple and therefore these viewers experienced no cognitive dissonance. Even so, Chan relates that audiences screamed when the couple kissed over the piano, because even though they knew it was really a man and a woman, at that point they had "bought" Wing as male. Revealing is that the film's primary audience (and the film's gaze) is heterosexual. While Leslie Cheung had a gay following, his primary fan base was straight female. For gays, Cheung undoubtedly became a symbol of gay pride, certainly after 1996. But one heterosexual Hong Kong filmgoer suggests that Hong Kong gays much prefer Stanley Kwan's drama *Lan Yu/Laam Yu/Lan Yu* (2001, starring Liu Ye and Hu Jun) over *He's a Woman* or Wong Kar-wai's *Happy Together/Chun gwong ja sit/Chun guang zha xie* (1997, also starring Cheung with Tony Leung Chiu-wai), with all of these films dealing with gay issues, while some members of the queer community feel both these films are not gay (read politically activist) enough. Most of the Hong Kong sexual minorities surveyed in this study preferred *Who's the Woman* over

He's a Woman. Considering Cheung's sexual ambiguity (see Chapters 3 and 4), it is worth noting that Hong Kongers generally, as a result of his so-called "coming out"/crossing over, either denied his behavior as idiosyncratic or labeled him as gay (despite his reportedly public comments that he was bisexual, and awareness in the queer community that Cheung was bisexual). It seems that sexual ambiguity left the former types of people at sea, and it was easier to use a binary opposition like straight or gay rather than confront the possibility of other or in-between sexual orientation.

One straight male spectator found the cross-dressing element "extremely weird" but most viewers found it innocuous, counterbalancing any threat with terms and phrases like "playful," "light-hearted," "harmless"; "comical," "funny," "it works and it's funny," "humorous"; "I don't mind," "it doesn't bother me," "I wasn't too bothered"; and, "no big deal." A 30-something female claims, "I responded with an open mind." A 20-something male says, "It doesn't bother me but it's something I would never do." One African-American female, on the other hand, complained, "The touching of hands by the gay characters and even the statements some of the characters made were disgusting." Another male confessed, "It raised my attention."

From a different and more open perspective, one 20-year-old Latino bisexual male, observes, "Hong Kong is very reserved when it comes to homosexuality and in China, under the communist regime, there has been the oppression of homosexuals. We are too accustomed to associating homosexuality with identity, as opposed to simply associating homosexuality with homosexual behavior. Why can some people only be something under the condition that they have certain genitalia?" A straight 21-year-old female adds, "The elements of cross-dressing do not surprise me nor are they something that I find strange, having quite a few gay friends and being around people who cross-dress is something quite natural and normal to me."

Young people today (mid-30s and under) have aged faster and earlier than in the past, having grown up under the process of globalization (see Chapter 4) where the pace of their everyday lives has rapidly accelerated. Their world picture includes Middle Eastern wars, terrorism, AIDS, consumerism, advanced technology, and pervasive mass media influence. Economic realities have resulted in shifting demographics with a more mobile population, but also the dissipation of nuclear family and loss of family networks, increased economic pressures with both parents (if present) working and often young people working themselves, at least part-time, once they are teens. As Benjamin R. Barber maps the globalization process, we face "Jihad vs. McWorld," with more centralized economic control by the multinational or global corporations and fragmented socio-political-cultural identity, leading to increased polarization and a growing underclass.[26] Rapidly advancing technology has provided convenience and instant gratification, which for all intents and purposes are taken for granted. While on the one hand, readily available and almost instantaneous communication is easier and cheaper and the world is a smaller place, on the other, the people in it are farther distanced by the intermediary conveniences technologies have been directed to provide, robbing us of human contact. The maturing generations of globalization are perhaps more confused than any previous generation, and adult as they may be, in some respects they are experiencing delayed development, particularly in defining themselves, their sexual orientations, and gender relations. Psychologist Erik Erikson observes that our sense of identity provides us with the ability to experience the self as something that has "continuity and sameness."[27]

But contemporary culture and selfhood are being shaped by discontinuity, difference, multiplicity, and gaps. Christian Metz's reflections on psychology and culture note the persistence of fantasies within film content, with film form itself as fantastic, and he points to identification as a precondition of fantasy.[28] Audiences find aspects of films with which to identify, whether character, star, action, situation, etc. but always through the lens of the camera (that is, already at one remove). A globalized perspective also contributes to the development of a pluralistic society, but diversity does not guarantee people will recognize and appreciate differences among cultural communities — i.e., queer communities. Especially in the US, the hegemony of individualism (i.e., my individualism, not necessarily the rights of the individual, conflated with consumer capitalism and a perverted identity — "you are what you buy") and a melting pot ethos lead to the opposite of tolerance, openness, and acceptance of other. Therefore, the ongoing actualization process of personal identity and authenticity for most of these heterosexual film-goers in this survey explains the xenophobic and sometimes homophobic responses provided.

Contested terrain theory grows out of Antonio Gramsci's conception of "cultural hegemony" and Michel Foucault's analysis of "discursive power."[29] It asserts that social values and practices are not fixed, but determined by the relative effectiveness of conflicting strategies adopted by the participants involved. Hegemony rests upon the apparent acceptability of the "dominant" way of life, with consent achieved through a network of mediating institutions, including popular culture and media, that "reproduce" existing modes and mores — i.e., a patriarchal society with heterosexual relationships. These become the "common sense" knowledge of everyday life. Mediation implies an absence of direct domination, however, and institutional "autonomy" provides opportunities to establish counter-hegemonic values and practices. Hence a mainstream movie like *He's a Woman, She's a Man*, despite its gender-bending and sexual ambiguity, achieved popularity among Hong Kong audiences and commercial success.

The French have an expression, "Plus ça change, plus la même chose (the more things change, the more they stay the same)" and it applies in the case of the majority of Hong Kong viewers in their reactions to *He's a Woman*. Cheng Yu described Cantonese 1950s and 60s audiences as having "identified themselves in the films, and that the films reflected their dreams, desires, and even, reality."[30] Not unlike American viewers of Busby Berkeley movies during the Great Depression, escaping their troubles through spectacle and identifying with the carefree and attractive wealthy, Hong Kong audiences, especially "ordinary people" could project themselves into the lifestyle of Sam (and Rose), believe in the fairy tale story and Wing's upward mobility in a transferred wish fulfillment, and also recognize the reality of Wing and Yu Lo's working class existence. No wonder Yuen became known as the "It Girl." Cheng also notes: "Cantonese comedy satisfied the escapist urge of the audience ... emphasizing the moral superiority of the poor and depicting the fantasy of a good life that would come with the shedding-off of poverty."[31] In some regards, Wing, for all her innocence, was seen as the acid test for judging the superficial relations that remain between Sam and Rose, but paradoxically they admired and imagined their lifestyle as their own. When Sam sees the error of his ways, not unlike the earlier characters that repented their unrighteous behavior, audiences were also able to forgive him his trespasses.

Chan himself described the first film as a "fantasy," and indeed, its happy ending reached to the film's box-office success, extended run, numerous awards, and popularity. The film won best actress for Yuen and best original song for "Chase" at the Hong Kong Film Awards, and was nominated for a slew of others, including best actor for Leslie Cheung, best new performer for Jordan Chan, and best director for Chan, as well as nominations for art direction, costume and make up, and best picture and screenplay. Chan was awarded best director and best film for 1994 by the Director's Guild of Hong Kong. The Hong Kong box-office take was approximately HK$29 million (US$3.75 million) [HK$29,131,628

(US$3,744,425)], and it was one of Hong Kong's top-grossers that year.[32] So the film Chan described as a "fantasy" had its own fairy tale happy ending with its success. Not so the sequel, *Who's the Woman*, which Chan characterizes as "an anti-statement of the first"; reality set in not only in the relationship story of Sam and Wing but in the film's reception.[33] Chan admits, "It made money, but it was not the kind of hit the studio wanted." For Chan, the first film was about "there is love ... love conquers all," and the second, "a relationship is a relationship ... that's reality, that's life." However, the sequel caused one 30-something South Korean heterosexual female to post the following: "At the end of the sequel, in the plane where they are off to Africa (I suppose references to Paul Simon and presumably *Graceland*) and all those other sonic signifiers for 'Africa' are another set of issues. Sam and Wing are in love again with their 'true' form, true selves, that is to say, so that the movie's happy ending underscores, or is resolved through the conventional heterosexual relationship. So for all the gender-bending, I wonder what Peter Chan's message is." A 20-something gay Hong Konger also questions, "[In *He's a Woman*], the Anita Yuen character should supposedly confuse him [Sam], but then he makes his final choice at last. I find this inconsistent, especially when we come to the sequel where Anita Mui, again confuses him." For both viewers, Chan's representation of both gender identity and sexual desire appears contradictory if not incompatible.

Generally, the majority of audiences were easily able to stomach the kisses between Leslie Cheung and Anita Yuen in the original film, knowing that the actors were male and female, cued by music and action that the sexual scenes between Anita Yuen and Carina Lau were played for laughs and easily dismissed, and that Eric Tsang was so over the top as to be perceived as non-threatening and comical (inoculation theory at work). In the sequel, however, the sexual scenes between Anita Yuen and Anita Mui were seriously and tenderly depicted even though Chan omits the details of their consummation, and we see them in bed, after the fact, learning that Wing has regrets while Fan Fan genuinely loves and desires her enough to give her up.[34] Even so, the sequel made conservative and straight audiences uneasy. Therefore, with the first film audiences experienced a pleasurable and fascinating crossing of boundaries as they watched the sexual scenes (with the question, "When will they all find out?" in their minds) whereas, in the sequel, the kiss and implied sex scene between Wing and Fan Fan gave no pleasure, and neither did the sex scene between Sam and Fan Fan.[35] There was no suspense, as there was nothing to be discovered, gender-wise, in terms of the three leads. One heterosexual male Hong Kong viewer dismisses the controversy, however, explaining, "The same sex kissing scene was not something new to me in 1994, as we all expected in a '90s Hong Kong film, anything would happen. That was an 'anything goes' moviemaking period."

Film reflects society and its values, according to Michael Parenti, who uses implant reinforcement theory to explain why people see what they do, no matter the intention of the filmmaker.[36] While *Who's the Woman?* was nominated for four Hong Kong film awards (for art direction, costume and makeup, best original song, and best new performer for Theresa Lee), there were no wins. The sequel's Hong Kong box-office take was approximately HK$21 million (US$2.5 million) [HK$20,916,798 (US$2,688,534)].[37] Chan allows, "It did pretty well at the box office, but nowhere close to the expectations." He continues, "When you make a movie, you can't really expect anything from the audience. People like it for different reasons, they see it at different levels ... When you've made a movie, your movie is not your movie anymore — it's theirs ... You can't tell them, 'But that's not what I meant.'" No matter a director's intention, films become what audiences make of them. Chan further admits that the gender-bending of the first film and its hot buttons were "non-intentional ... I didn't realize the impact until I saw it." The sequel can be understood as a culturally radical affirmation of gender difference working within the confines of mainstream (and heteronormative) cinema, and therefore both disruptive and subversive, opening space and power for marginalized sexualities and gendering. The subtle ambiguities analyzed throughout this study "disturb stable definitions" and encourage "queer representation" both onscreen and in perception.[38] For a heterosexual audience, this can mean reaching into their own repressed desires and through fantasy indulging what they may perceive as sexual taboos as defined by their society, without disrupting it.[39]

Chan reflects, "The fact that there are aspects of gender-bending and homosexuality issues in Chinese opera and the movies doesn't make the society more liberal. The society is very conservative, probably more conservative than here [US]. The difference is, I think, the art in Hong Kong or Asia doesn't reflect the general society as much as here. I think because of the studio system ... Everything in this country is based on opinion, research, recruited audience, stuff like that ... Investors are usually pretty gutless. You make films, you don't make films that will intimidate or offend the audience. Because we don't have tools and do that research in Asia. You just go make them. You realize after you make them that people take things much more liberally in movies [and you can] offend them but it doesn't really. It doesn't really change their views on issues in life. Personally, I think Asian or Hong Kong society is much more conservative than in the US." Chan, therefore, seems to dismiss the potential social effect of his films. On the other hand, comedic screenwriter, actor, and director Li Heng, whose career in Cantonese movies spanned more than 20 years, explains, "film is a tool for education. Making films is quite distinct from running a grocery store. The number of people who will be influenced by your work is a thousand times more. Therefore, a film producer should have a sense of social responsibility."[40] Gerald Mast notes, "Even the most lighthearted, escapist piece of fun inevitably implies serious values. The audience, however, might fully understand the comedy without examining any of its values; and the artist (or artisan) might not care whether anyone can find a serious implication in it, might not even know what values he used to build it ... this kind [of comedy] only implies values, and it may make no difference to the comic effect whether the audience sees those implications or not."[41] Mast seems to concur with Chan on this point, suggesting the limited potential of film to change us, and I believe, underestimates audiences' emotional and intellectual responses to the medium and the power of laughter.

Consider the following from this study: "The movie challenges the status quo yet manages to reaffirm its underlying values." Or, from a more mature female describing herself as between 35 and 40: "Chan is taking a risk and a stand by giving depth to the movie storyline in order for [a member of] his audience to grow inside as a person and to make people realize that our world is constantly changing. We as individuals and as a nation need to respect and love each other as human beings. I loved the in-depth look at how we as human beings question ourselves, our lives, and make sense out of it all. No matter your sexual orientation, we are all human beings who essentially need the same things in life to survive and live a happy life." Another describing himself as "omnisexual" took the film more personally, explaining, "I intuit that Chan's intentional message in this sexual comedy of errors is the relativity of sexuality and when all is said and done and the lights go out, WHO THE HELL CARES. And I am not an exponent of free love but living out my sexuality as the desk of destiny deals my hand ... Everything I said I would never do, I've done, so I have no shame in that respect nor regrets." A Hong Kong viewer remarks, "If Peter Chan hadn't made *Comrades Almost a Love Story, He's a Woman, She's a Man* would definitely be his one film to be remembered, plus UFO's best." The film's ironies, uncertainties, and contradictions open it up for audience interaction and further discussion. By problematizing gender identities and sexual orientations and presenting numerous aspects of contemporary globalization, Chan challenges heteronormative and traditional values and destabilizes current practices of global capitalism in two ways — 1) by paradoxically making a commercially successful mainstream film that capitalizes on a commercially driven industry supported by local profiteers and exploited globally, and 2) by selling commodities — styles, people, products, and a fantasy life — but simultaneously exploring the commodification of almost everything and creating a unique hybrid local not for sale that reaches an audience. He does not exactly preach and tell us what to think, but the way that *He's a Woman* and *Who's the Woman* are structured, nudges us along to indeed consider. He targets the mainstream and thereby reaches a larger audience in a humorous and touching way in a progressive film. Not radical, not art house, not independent cinema, but the commercial entertainment it was meant to be.

Notes

Chapter 1   Comedy and More

1   Personal interviews, 8 October and 18 December 1998. All future Chan quotations are taken from these interviews unless otherwise noted.

2   See Chan's basic biographical information at http://www.hkcinemagic. com/en/people.asp?id=9 or under "People" at the website of Chan's current company, Applause Pictures, at www.applausepictures.com.

3   Most audiences are clued in to this fact, especially in Hong Kong, where pop singers also "cross over" into the film industry, becoming actors. Many, like Leslie Cheung, continue working in both industries. But for those unaware, Chan offers a clue later in the film, where Sam is reading the book *Film Music*, whose title is clearly readable in both English and Chinese.

4   Peter Bogdanovich, *Peter Bogdanovich's Movie of the Week: 52 Classic Films for One Full Year* (New York: Ballantine Books, 1999), p. 138. Similarly, veteran actor Cary Grant also acknowledged, "Comedy holds the greatest risk for an actor, and the laughter is the reward." Quoted in Geoffrey Wansell, *Cary Grant: Dark Angel* (New York: Arcade, 1996), p. 47.

5   Henri Bergson, *Laughter: An Essay on the Meaning of the Comic*, trans. Cloudesley Brereton and Fred Rothwell (New York: MacMillian Company, 1914), p. 2.

6   Logan Hill, "Steve Carell's Smokin'! But He'd Rather Not Fan His Own Flames," *New York*, 31 July–7 August 2006: 68.

7   Gerald Mast, *The Comic Mind: Comedy and the Movies,* 2nd ed. (Chicago: University of Chicago Press, 1979), p. 4. Note: Mast's text discusses mostly Hollywood comedies pre-1980, but his typology is useful for evaluating comedy.

8   Ibid., p. 6.

9   Ibid.

10   Ibid., pp. 8–9.

11   Although contemporary Hong Kong films mix distinctive elements of various genres in the same film (this to satisfy all audiences' tastes, not unlike Shakespeare's theater), in some respects to assign genres is not as good a fit as in other cinemas, but movies generally are identified by film-goer by known genres — i.e., John Woo's action cinema, Jackie Chan's action comedy, etc. Most of Chan's films have been "dramedies," with comedy dominant; *Comrades, Almost a Love Story/Tim mat mat/Tian mi mi* (1996) is just the opposite — drama with some comedic elements.

12   Screwball's origins vary. Basically "one or both of the leads is a 'screwball,' an 'oddball whose unconventional nature is responsible for the equally unconventional situations in which the characters find themselves," Bernard F. Dick, *Anatomy of Film* (Boston: Bedford Books, 2005), pp. 145–54, and so named because of "the wild, out of control baseball pitch." Maria Pramaggiore and Tom Wallis, *Film: A Critical Introduction* (Boston: Pearson Education, 2006), pp. 359–60.

13   Stanley Cavell, *Pursuits of Happiness: The Hollywood Comedy of Remarriage* (Cambridge: Harvard University Press, 1981). Cavell cites Howard Hawks's *Bringing Up Baby* (1938) as an example of the first, and George Cukor's *Philadelphia Story* (1940) as an example of the second. Chan's first film, described as a "fantasy," and the sequel as "reality," echo Cavell's description.

14   To wit, Chan's combination of comedy and drama is delicately balanced, having the best of both worlds. Consider this male spectator's

response, a reaction to the story's dramatic elements and theme: "The movie to me seemed very sad most of the way through. You have a pathetic 20-something year-old kid idealizing these two superstars that lead cover lives to keep their image. Deeper into the story I started to see the message that love has no boundaries, including gender. That a homophobic man such as Cheung's character can fall in love with what he believes is a man is the true definition of love in my eyes, a feeling from one person to another with no prejudice. This is why I think it is a good love story, maybe not the most romantic but still a really good love story." Further audience responses throughout include, but are not limited to, students from Seminole Community College, Sanford, Florida, US, in World Cinema and Art of Film classes, in which the movie was watched, 2005–2008, with students ranging in age from 18–70. Other responses come from various classes taught over the last ten years, as well as international students from the Pacific Islands, various Latin American countries, and the Caribbean (including Mexico, Venezuela, Peru, Colombia, Argentina, Nicaragua, Cuba, and Puerto Rico), Canada, Japan, and South Korea, as well as non-student Hong Kongers outside the film industry, American Koreans and Chinese, and anonymous sources from various Internet communities. Sexual orientation varies but is primarily heterosexual.

15   "Love Hong Kong Film," 30 September 2005, http://www.lovehkfilm. com/reviews/hes_a_woman_shes_a_man.htm.

16   "Love Hong Kong Film."

17   The late star Leslie Cheung described working with Chan and the film as follows: "Cela a été une expérience assez intéressante, de travailler avec Peter Chan ... Le film de Peter Chan pose le problème de l'identité sexuelle. Le film est très drôle, sans être calculé." Michel Ciment and Hubert Niogret, "Entretien Leslie Cheung: Dix-huit ans de travail acharne," *Positif* 455 (January 1999): 99.

18   Betsy Sherman, unpublished taped interview with Peter Chan; Sherman's review appeared as "Opening *The Love Letter*," *Boston Globe*, 16 May 1999: N9+.

19   See Ackbar Abbas, *Hong Kong: Culture and the Politics of Disappearance* (Minneapolis: University of Minnesota Press, 1997)

on Hong Kong as a city of presence and absence, recognizing but also destroying the past as it moves into the future.

20   Recently, Chan paid homage to the Hong Kong musicals popular in the 1960s, with the release of his musical *Perhaps Love/Ruoguo ai/ Aiqing* (2005).

21   Ng Ho, "A Preliminary Plot Analysis of Cantonese Comedy," in The 9th Hong Kong International Film Festival, *The Traditions of Hong Kong Comedy* (Hong Kong: Urban Council, 1985), p. 24.

22   Stephen Teo, "Genre, Authorship, and Articulation," in The 9th Hong Kong International Film Festival, *The Traditions of Hong Kong Comedy* (Hong Kong: Urban Council, 1985), p. 89.

23   See John Morreall, *Taking Laughter Seriously* (New York: SUNY University Press, 1983).

24   Mast, p. 27.

25   Bergson, pp. 7–8.

26   Ibid., p. 19.

27   Stephen Teo uses this proverb, translated as "to evoke the past so as to inherit its legacy," in his discussion of Allen Fong's *Father and Son/Fuzi Qing* (1981) in relation to its predecessors Ng Wui's *Father and Son/Fuzi Qing* (1954) and Chun Kim's *Parents' Hearts/Fumu Xin* (1955). See Teo, *Hong Kong Cinema: The Extra Dimensions* (London: BFI Publishing, 1997), p. 62. Andrew Grossman borrows from Teo in his discussion of Yim Ho's *Kitchen* (1997), explaining it as "the invocation and subsumption of the past for the good of the future." See Grossman, "The Rise of Homosexuality and the Dawn of Communism in Hong Kong Film: 1993–1998," in Andrew Grossman, ed., *Queer Asian Cinema: Shadows in the Shade* (New York: Harrington Park Press, 2000), pp. 172–74.

28   Cheng Yu, "The World According to Everyman," in The 9th Hong Kong International Film Festival, *The Traditions of Hong Kong Comedy* (Hong Kong: Urban Council, 1985), p. 41.

29   Law Kar, "A Comparative Analysis of Cantonese and Mandarin Comedies," in The 9th Hong Kong International Film Festival, *The Traditions of Hong Kong Comedy* (Hong Kong: Urban Council, 1985), p. 14.

30   Ibid., pp. 15–16.

31   Ng, pp. 21–26.

32 Ibid., pp. 22–25.

33 Law Kar, "Broker La, Gao Xiong and Mo Kangshi," in The 9th Hong Kong International Film Festival, *The Traditions of Hong Kong Comedy* (Hong Kong: Urban Council, 1985), p. 53.

34 Cheng, p. 44.

35 Ibid., p. 45.

36 Ibid., p. 42.

37 The Chinese title was previously used in Hong Kong for the title of two films, the first being the Cantonese title given William Wyler's *Roman Holiday* (1953), starring Audrey Hepburn and Gregory Peck. (Hepburn plays a spoiled and reluctant princess who takes a holiday from her position; Peck is the reporter on to her truancy. Although she eventually rises to the occasion and returns to her responsibilities, she announces, remembering her "holiday," she will "cherish the memory as long as I live.") The other, a 1964 Shaoxing opera film comedy (similar in style to the popular *huangmei* opera) released by Great Wall and starring Miranda Yang (Xia Meng) and an all-female cast, included a "male" character disguising himself as a female in order to test the young woman he admires. (The same opera served as another *huangmei diao* film made in Taiwan in 1974, and starred Ivy Ling Po and Sylvia Chang). The above surely illustrates Chan as the link between past and future, with him drawing on opera and film for his movie. Personal correspondence, Terence Chang and Law Kar, 14 April 2007 and 20 April 2007, respectively.

38 "A Good Year," *Entertainment Weekly* (Fall Movie Preview 2006): 79.6 .

Chapter 2   Camera, Sound, and Music

1 Quoted from an unpublished Betsy Sherman taped interview with Peter Chan; Sherman's review drawing on her interview was published as "Opening *The Love Letter*," *Boston Globe*, 16 May 1999: N9+.

2 Ibid.

3 Quoted in *I Lived, But...* , a 1983 documentary on Ozu by Kuzuo Inoue and featuring actors Chishu Ryu, Mariko Okada, and Haruko

Sugimura, director (and former assistant) Shohei Imamura, and film
critics Donald Ritchie and Tadao Sato. The documentary is included
on the Criterion Collection DVD release of *Tokyo Story*, 2003.

4   See, for example, Gilles Neret, *Tamara de Lempicka 1898–1980* (Koln:
Benedikt Taschen, 1992), p. 8; Alain Blondel, et al., *Tamara de
Lempicka Art Deco Icon* (London: Royal Academy of the Arts, 2004),
pp. 33, 55; and numerous references in the biography by Laura
Claridge, *Tamara de Lempicka: A Life of Deco and Decadence* (New
York: Clarkson Potter, 1999).

5   English subtitles provided by Hong Kong product have improved, but
are often inaccurate. Translation provided by former student Jamie
Wong Hei-kwan, a former Hong Kong native currently residing in the
US.

6   See Chan's revelation from personal experience in Chapter 3, regarding
his being mistaken for a woman.

7   Bruce Jay Friedman's 1962 black humor novel *Stern* expresses this
idea best: "A kiss is an upper persuasion for a lower invasion."

8   Gerald Mast, *The Comic Mind: Comedy and the Movies*, 2nd ed.
(Chicago: University of Chicago Press, 1979), pp. 11–12.

Chapter 3   Cross-Dressing, Gender-Bending, and Sexual Orientation

1   Gerald Mast, *The Comic Mind: Comedy and the Movies*, 2nd ed.
(Chicago: University of Chicago Press, 1979), p. 21.

2   That such distinctions have entered the mainstream, at least in the
US, is evidenced by the recently released *I Now Pronounce You Chuck
and Larry* (2007), a Hollywood comedy directed by Dennis Dugan
and starring Adam Sandler and Kevin James. The two stars play New
York firefighters who pose as a gay couple to insure domestic partner
benefits. Television promotionals include a voice-over announcing,
"Chuck and Larry are not gay ... but everyone has to think they are"
with teasers between the characters like, "I can't be gay for you, Larry.
I can be a lesbian, but that's about it," and "We're gay, not
transsexuals."

3   Homi K. Bhabba, *The Location of Culture* (London: Routledge, 1994), p. 1.

4   Siu-leung Li, *Cross-Dressing in Chinese Opera* (Hong Kong: Hong Kong University Press, 2003), p. 1.

5   Ibid., p. 40.

6   Ibid., pp. 19, 40.

7   Ng Ho, "A Preliminary Plot Analysis of Cantonese Comedy," in The 9th Hong Kong International Film Festival, *The Traditions of Hong Kong Comedy* (Hong Kong: Urban Council, 1985), p. 21.

8   Pang Chai-choi and Lin Li, "Portraits of Ten Comedians," in The 9th Hong Kong International Film Festival, *The Traditions of Hong Kong Comedy* (Hong Kong: Urban Council, 1985), p. 61.

9   Mast, p. 4.

10   For "the male gaze," see Laura Mulvey's influential *Screen* article (1979) included in *Visual and Other Pleasures* (Bloomington: Indiana University Press, 1989), pp. 14–26. For the "heterosexual division of the universe," see Judith Mayne, *Women at the Keyhole: Feminism and Women's Cinema* (Bloomington: Indiana University Press, 1990), p. 118.

11   In the latter, based on a Ming dynasty folk tale, a male scholar falls for a fellow scholar revealed to be a woman who has disguised herself as male so that she may study; it served as the basis for the Chinese opera *Why Not Return?* (*Hu bugui?*).

12   Andrew Grossman, "The Rise of Homosexuality and the Dawn of Communism in Hong Kong Film: 1993–1998," in Andrew Grossman, ed., *Queer Asian Cinema: Shadows in the Shade* (New York: Harrington Park Press, 2000), p. 162. (The other film to which Grossman alludes is Tsui Hark's *The Lovers*).

13   Feng Luo, *City on the Edge of Time/Sheng shi bian yuan: Xianggang dian ying de xing bie te ji yu qui zheng zhi* (Hong Kong: Oxford University Press, 2002), pp. 29–42. Similar to Luo's comment regarding art and life performance, one viewer observes, "Cheung was in a sense a private person living a public life" in relation to his sexual orientation.

14   Quoted in Kwan's *Yang ± Yin: Gender in Chinese Cinema* (*Nan sheng nu xiang: Zhongguo dianying zhi xingbie*, 1996).

15   Marjorie Garber, *Vested Interests: Cross-Dressing and Cultural Anxiety* (New York: Harper Collins, 1992), p. 184.
16   Rebecca Bell-Metereau, *Hollywood Androgyny*, 2nd ed. (New York: Columbia University Press, 1993), p. xix.
17   This combination is reinforced in the role reversal of Sam and Wing in the sequel, which delivers the one-two punch of public man–private woman. Sam is the stay-at-home worrier, a bit tetchy, while Wing "brings home the bacon."
18   A representative sampling of typical responses from viewers follows:
     "I don't think this film is attempting to reinforce stereotypes; it's making light of them."
     "Comedic and entertaining, but kind of overplayed."
     "[Eric Tsang's portrayal] may be offensive to some people, but funny to most."
     "There is definitely gay stereotyping in the film, but its effects are harmless and comedic. I responded with admiration to the clever use of it. I thought that the way it was handled is so light that it's tasteful and artful, especially for such a touchy topic."
     "[The gay stereotyping was] done very well with a touch of sensitivity and lightheartedness."
     "There certainly are all sorts of stereotypes here — the flamey Auntie with his hip-swaying walk, the way he talked (inflections of voice), his arm and hand motions; the gay character [Joseph/Josephine (Law Kar-ying)] playing classical piano (Mozart Sonata in C Major) and his unbridled libido, his apparent obsession with penises, etc.; and, Fish teaching Wing how to walk ('walk, walk, scratch')."
     "As for the effects of gay stereotyping, well, the usual: Sam becomes intimidated by Wing and avoids being nude, or exposed in front of 'him,' while many still avoid other homosexual encounters throughout the film."
19   Tsang would reprise a gay characterization, without the caricature, deeper and more dramatic, in Stanley Kwan's *Hold You Tight/Yue faai lok yue doh laai/Yu kuai le yu duo luo* (1998).
20   See James B. Stiff and Paul A. Mongeau, *Persuasive Communication*, 2nd ed. (New York: Guilfrod Press, 2003), pp. 286–94. Inoculation theory was defined by William McGuire and the theory came into

wide use in the 1960s. I am also indebted to my colleague Bobbie Bell at Seminole Community College for practical applications of the strategy.

21 Judith Butler, *Bodies That Matter: On the Discursive Limits of "Sex"* (New York: Routledge, 1990), p. 95.

22 Mast, p. 11.

23 Regarding this scene, "Do men not live in houses?" asks one spectator.

24 Luo, pp. 29–42.

25 Although perhaps not, as two queer perspectives have described her cross-dressing as "transgendered," in one instance, and "transvestite" in another.

26 Here is a range of audience responses, running the gamut:

"It is Leslie Cheung's portrayal of Sam that holds the most meaning. Both Rose and Wing are set in heterosexual archetypes even if one is more of an androgynous figure. Sam, on the other hand, throughout the movie and even until the end is a confused and overly insecure character. His problem with accepting his sexual preference makes him a character to feel for. Sure, Rose is shunted to the side, but in life any relationship can't work out without compatibility. Sam's gradual 'dropping' of Rose can be seen in the context of the film as not so much a deliberately malevolent gesture, but one out of uncertainty where his path in life truly lies. Also, the one comment of Rose's on being very possessive (she will do anything to keep him) mirrors the obsession Wing has with their relationship. And Wing perhaps is the driving force that helps us to understand Sam's conflict. Although we the audience know Wing is in fact female, the fact that her alternate visage brings up feelings of homosexuality, even at the end when Sam finds out she is a woman, his line 'man or woman, it doesn't matter, all I know is that I love you,' shows that ultimately for Sam, love is not defined by gender but by what lies within the heart. In terms of societal norms, if Wing was in fact a man, we couldn't argue against Sam's feelings and intentions, but if we step out of that context, Sam can be seen as a loving, caring person who craves real love, a true mental, physical, and spiritual connection, not just physical attraction, which in my opinion makes him the true hero and most relatable character in Chan's film."

"Is Peter Chan homosexual? Where can I get a copy of this film?"

"I can see how this very interesting movie could make some people very uncomfortable. It could make some men question their own sexuality, with the male character [Sam] questioning himself like that. I think many people may have caught themselves mixing up gender, especially with little kids. Most parents have had to deal with people calling their girls boys or their boys girls. So, are there really big differences between men and women? Well, the differences are pretty much hormonally and chemically. We produce pheromones that attract the opposite sex and hormones control the menstrual cycle. As for the two female characters having their [sexual] moment and the younger character wanting to touch the other woman's breasts, I think that is totally normal. People are often curious of something unusual to them and I think it is perfectly normal for men and women to admire people of the same sex and even to be able to pick out an attractive person of the same sex."

"Does the movie critique Hong Kong society's reception to gay people? Sam's shame and torment when he finds himself attracted to Wing, and his thinking that this truth will hurt his image and status in the Hong Kong entertainment industry and then his finally accepting this in the name of 'true love' seem to steer in this direction."

27   Numerous Shakespeare scholars have noted that in *Hamlet*, Hamlet returns from sea, saved from death by pirates, a changed man, more stoical and at peace, ready to accept what is to come. See, for example, scholars such as Harold Bloom, James Calderwood, Jan Kott, Stephen Greenblatt, Sidney Homan, and Jan Kott, to mention only a few.

28   Grossman, p. 162.

29   See Michel Foucault, *The History of Sexuality: Volume 1: An Introduction*, trans. Robert Hurley (New York: Vintage, 1976, 1990), and George Chauncey, *Gay New York: Gender, Urban Culture, and the Making of the Gay Male World 1890–1940* (New York: Basic Books 1994).

30   Siu-leung Li, *Cross-Dressing in Chinese Opera* (Hong Kong: Hong Kong University Press, 2003), p. 31. Li cites Robert Hans Van Gulik's study *Sexual Life in Ancient China: A Preliminary Study of Chinese Sex and Society from ca. 1500 B.C. till 1644 A.D.* (Leiden: E. J. Brill, 1961).

31 Lionel Ovesey, *Homosexuality and Pseudohomosexuality* (New York: Science House, 1969). See also Ethel Spector Person, *The Sexual Century* (New Haven, Connecticut: Yale University Press, 1999).

32 The Stonewall Riots are so named because of the place where they began, the Stonewall Inn in New York City's Greenwich Village. In the early hours of 28 June 1969, police raided the club, rounding up non-heterosexuals of many persuasions, leading to an outbreak of several days of demonstrations and riots. Stonewall marks the beginning of gays fighting back against persecution and actively organizing, that is, the beginning of Gay Liberation or the Gay Rights movement in the US. For gay film studies, see Richard Dyer, ed., *Gays and Film* (London: BFI, 1977).

33 Vito Russo, *The Celluloid Closet: Homosexuality in the Closet* (New York: Harper & Row, 1981).

34 Richard Barrios, *Screened Out: Playing Gay in Hollywood From Edison to Stonewall* (New York: Routledge, 2005).

35 See *Queer Cinema, The Film Reader*, ed. Harry Benshoff and Sean Griffin (New York: Routledge, 2004). As a part of the "In Focus Routledge Film Readers," the anthology dispels any simplistic notions of gendering and provides a history of queer cinematic representation as well as an overview of the theoretical models used to analyze cinematic representation.

36 See Judith Halberstam, *In a Queer Time and Place: Transgender Bodies, Subcultural Lives* (New York: New York University Press, 2005); Jay Prosser, *Second Skins: The Body Narratives of Transsexuality* (New York: Columbia University Press, 1998); and Diana Fuss, *Identification Papers* (New York: Routledge, 1995).

37 See Judith Butler, *Gender Trouble: Feminism and the Subversion of Identity* (New York: Routledge, 1990) and *Bodies That Matter: On the Discursive Limits of "Sex"* (New York: Routledge, 1990).

38 See Foucault, above, and *The History of Sexuality, Volume 1: An Introduction*; *Volume II: The Use of Pleasure*; and, *Volume III: The Care of the Self.* The first volume was published in French in 1976 and translated into English in 1977. The latter two volumes were both published in French in 1984, and translated into English in 1985 and 1986 respectively.

39 Helen Hok-sze Leung, "Queerscapes in Contemporary Hong Kong Cinema," *Positions* 9:2 (Fall 2001): 423–47. See Ingram's essay "Marginality and the Landscapes of Erotic Alien(nations)," in *Queers in Space: Communities, Public Places, Sites of Resistance*, ed. Anne-Marie Bouthillette, Yolanda Retter, and Gordon Brent Ingram (Seattle: Bay Press, 1997), pp. 27–52.

40 On the other hand, following the June 3rd–4th 1989 Tiananmen Square crackdown, one million (one in six) Hong Kongers protested and held vigil in solidarity with the Mainland's student pro-democracy movement (known as the June 4th Movement). And surely on the minds of many was the impending return of Hong Kong to the Mainland. Since 1989, thousands of Hong Kongers have gathered on June 4th every year in Victoria Park, holding a candlelight vigil to commemorate the victims of the massacre. See CNN news coverage at http://www.cnn.com/WORLD/9706/04/tiananmen.hong.kong/#1. See also Hong Kong novelist Sussy Chakó's/Xu Xi's description of the events following Tiananmen in her short story "Danny's Snake": "And then, he told her about the miles of demonstrators, how beautiful and terrible this outpouring was, previously so repressed. People from all walks of life marched into the streets to confront the inevitable change to the status quo, whatever the change would bring. Was it fear, she asked, and perhaps humiliation at their helplessness, their loss of control? No, he replied, people were angry and outraged, not afraid, more indignant than humiliated. It was a protest, a demand to be heard. It was unlike anything he had ever seen in Hong Kong." Sussy Chakó/Xu Xi, *Daughters of Hui* (Hong Kong: Asia 2000 Limited, 1996), p. 28.

Furthermore, since the return, there have been numerous pro-democracy/anti-dictatorship rallies and demonstrations, ranging from the 50,000-person protest in 2003 against passage of "anti-subversion" laws that would restrict civic freedoms to the 250,000 marchers in December 2005 who remonstrated against a proposal that would delay the introduction of a one man–one vote system. While Hong Kongers may be categorized as apolitical, there are cultural and film industry figures who are politically active, such as actor/producer John Shum Kin-fun, a visible and vocal political activist in Hong Kong's pro-democracy movement. There are similarities between Hong Kong's pro-democracy groups, which mushroomed following Tiananmen Square in 1989 and continued to expand with the first direct elections to the Legislative Council in 1991 [groups include both actual political parties and lawmakers as well as social activists and civil organizations, among them, the Democratic Party (Martin Lee), People Pile, April Fifth Action (Leung Kwok-hung, known as "Longhair"), The Frontier, Civil Act Up, and queer communities]; both the activists and queer groups agree on the issues but disagree on the ways and means of achieving their goals.

41 The pervasiveness of anti-homosexual sentiment in Hong Kong can be seen in remarks made during the discussion that took place during the Hong Kong Legislative Council's meeting regarding the Crimes (Amendment) Bill that effectively decriminalized homosexuality.

Some remarks acknowledged the homophobic taboo as dominant, applauding the Council for what it was about to enact:

Mr. James David McGregor, OBE, ISO, JP: "Hong Kong people seem to regard male homosexuality as an unmentionable aberration from normal social behavior, so much so that many local people have claimed that homosexuality is a western preference and has little to do with Chinese society. Family and parental attitudes in Hong Kong have never been able to accept the changing patterns and recognition of the wide differences in sexuality and sexual preferences which have come to light in modern times. This Council has reached, or will shortly do, a brave decision to disregard what may be in fact the majority view in Hong Kong. We have given relief to many male homosexuals who will no longer have to fear prosecution and persecution against the state that God created them in. Some of the world's most brilliant men were and are homosexuals. God created them too."

Other remarks reinstated homophobia and homophobia as an acceptable societal taboo. Note that the response below contradicts the historically documented conventional practice of homosexuality in parts of China (discussed later in this chapter) and also that the above response accurately describes the position below:

Mr. Kingsley Sit Ho-yin: "Members all know that the public is disposed against decriminalization of homosexuality ... The legalization, or decriminalization, of homosexuality is contrary to the moral standards of traditional Chinese society."

See the record through the Hong Kong government's official website at http://www.legco.gov.hk /yr90-91/english/lc_sitg/hansard/ h910710.pdf.

42 In discussing gay director Edward Lam and his homoerotic piece *Scenes From a Man's Changing Room*, staged by Zuni Icosahedron a month after Hong Kong decriminalized homosexuality in June 1991, Rozanna Lilley uses an old Cantonese expression, "hek ye ge laigau" or "the customs and traditions that devour people" to describe Lam's feelings expressed by the play. She quotes an interview in the 1 January 1991 *Sing Pao Daily*, in which Lam states, "I feel I am a marginal man. I find that I do not identify with men under the traditional standard. Those type of men represent ignorance and power worship. However, I can feel the feeling of safety when I am with them. I feel confused. I intend to express my understanding of my sexuality from the perspective of being contradictory in my feeling and thinking." See Rozanna Lilley, *Staging Hong Kong: Gender and Performance in Transition* (Honolulu: University of Hawai'i Press, 1998), pp. 8–9.

43 June Lam, "Leslie Cheung's '98 Declaration: An Interview before the Golden Horse Awards," *City Entertainment* 491 (5–13 February 1998): 11–16. I had the pleasure of lunching with June Lam during the symposium "The Film Scene: Cinema, the Arts, and Social Change" held by the University of Hong Kong, 21–22 April 2006.

44 In contrast, director Stanley Kwan came out onscreen to his mother while filming *Yang ± Yin: Gender in Chinese Cinema* (*Nan sheng nu xiang: Zhongguo dianying zhi xingbie*, 1996). Previously, Kwan was known as a "women's director," coded language for gay, as with other directors like George Cukor.

45 Cheung was interviewed just before the gala premiere of *From Ashes to Ashes* (2000), a short film he directed, co-wrote, and co-starred in, and produced for RTHK (Radio Television Hong Kong) and the Hong Kong Council on Smoking and Health to support an anti-smoking campaign. Cheung saw the film, after all his success, as a way of giving back to the people of Hong Kong. But he commented on the difference

between reel and real life at that time, and the observation is eerie considering his suicide on 1 April 2003. "What's most important," he says, looking straight into the camera, "is that we can always get second takes in acting, in reel life, but there's only one take in real life."

46   "Love HK Film," 20 May 2004, http://www.brns.com/hkactors/pages/page23.html.

47   By the "Passion Tour," Cheung had released the album *Big Heat* (2000), which included the song "Me", aka "I am what I am," the lyrics penned by popular (and sexually ambiguous) writer Lin Xi. Many gay audiences took the song as Cheung's "coming out" both with the release (recorded in Cantonese and Mandarin) and in performance. Selective lyrics follow. "I am what I am. I am me, such a special me.../ With my heart, telling the world what courage is.../ What am I? I'm a miracle.../ I'm living as a human being shamelessly/ Telling the world what courage is" (Cantonese version). "I am what I am. I will forever love this 'me'.../ No need to hide. Living for the kind of life that I like/ No need to paint or decorate. Just stand there in the bright corner/ I am me. The fire light of a different color.../ Living happily in a glass house, telling the world/ What it is to be living in the light, shamelessly" (Mandarin version).

48   One spectator, discussing men cross-dressing as women, comments: "I will end by quoting Mae West on female impersonation. 'What's wrong? Women have been doing it for years.'"

49   Travis S. K. Wong, "Queering Masculinities in Hong Kong Movies," in *Masculinities and Hong Kong Cinema*, ed. Lai-kwan Pang and Day Wong (Hong Kong: Hong Kong University Press, 2005), p. 63. See also Jason Ho Ka-hang's reinterpretation and defense of Stanley Kwan and *The Island Tales* as queer (re)evaluation in Jason Ho Ka-hang, "A Queer (Re)evaluation: Stanley Kwan and The Island Tales," at *Cultural Studies Monthly*, 18 June 2007, http://www.cc.ncu.edu.tw/~csa/journal/64/journal_park476.htm.

50   Grossman, p. 162.

51   Ibid., p. 163.

52   I am freely adapting Freud's notion of "the uncanny," as first developed in a paper of the same title, published in 1919. Included in "The Uncanny" in *The Standard Edition of the Complete Psychological*

Works of Sigmund Freud. Vol. XVII (1917–1919), trans. James Strachey, et al. (London: Hogarth Press, 1955), pp. 217–52.

53 William Empson, *Seven Types of Ambiguity*, 3rd ed. (London: Chatto & Windus, 1963).

54 Ibid., p. 155.

55 Ibid., p. 192.

56 Says Chan, "I'm a very contradictory person when it comes to what we believe in. I do believe that somehow everything is taking a course that is chartered and planned, especially when it comes to relationships. If it's yours, it's yours. If it's not, it's not." Note Chan's explanation of relationships is gender non-specific.

57 Grossman, pp. 163–64.

58 Bell-Metereau, p. xiii. Leslie Cheung himself presented a sexually ambiguous figure, having publicly stated he was bisexual, but being perceived by many others as gay or idiosyncratic.

59 Ed Sikov, *Laughing Hysterically: American Screen Comedy of the 1950s* (New York: Columbia University Press, 1994), p. 118.

60 Kwai-cheung Lo, *Chinese Face/Off: The Transnational Popular Culture of Hong Kong* (Urbana: University of Illinois Press, 2005), p. 118.

61 I am grateful to Jason Ho Ka-hang for bringing this reading to my attention; we met at the University of Hong Kong's symposium "The Film Scene: Cinema, the Arts, and Social Change," held in Spring 2006. The symposium included an enlightening session entitled "The Queer Scene," and pun intended, queer presence was visible and vocal, not only with participants and the selection of papers on a variety of films (not just at this session), but also with information shared about the Hong Kong Lesbian & Gay Film and Video Festival, active since 1989, presented by Denise Tang.

62 Lilley, p. 213.

63 Mary Wong Shuk-han, "The Struggles of Sexual Orientation — On Three Hong Kong Films in 1998 [Xingxiang de jiaoli — lun jiu nian san chu Xianggang dianying de changshi]," in *Contemporary Chinese Cinema: 1998 [Dangdai Zhongguo dianying: yi jiu jiu ba]*, ed. Huang Wulan (Taipei: Shi bao wenhua chuban qiye gufen youxiangongsi, 1999), p. 112. Cited by Jason Ho Ka-hang, "Reinterpreting a Queer

Experience: A Study of Stanley Kwan's Films and Their Reception," unpublished thesis, University of Hong Kong, 2006, p. 9.

64   In Mainland China, Criminal Law No. 106 states: "All revolting behaviors should be subjected to arrest and sentence." Homosexuality, although denied as even existing, since there is no reference in the Criminal Code, is paradoxically regarded as one type of revolting behavior. There are provisions for punishment, ranging from public condemnation to police harassment and institutionalization. Cited by Lilley, pp. 219–20.

65   Grossman, p. 153.

66   "Chinese Checkers: The Great Wall shatters H'wood's hopes for pic blitz," *Variety*, 17–23 July 2006: 50.

67   Mast, p. 340.

68   Ibid., p. 22.

69   Ibid., p. 23.

Chapter 4   Commerce and Globalization

1   Nick Browne, "Introduction," in *New Chinese Cinemas: Forms, Identities, Politics*, ed. Nick Browne, et al. (Cambridge: Cambridge University Press, 1994), p. 7.

2   "Film Entertainment Services," 8 July 1997, http://www.info.gov.hk.

3   Once producing approximately 250 films a year, Hong Kong's "production output has dropped to 50 films annually." Vicki Rothrock, "Gov't mulls how to aid Hong Kong filmmakers," *Variety*, 23–29 April 2007: 9.

4   See Sheldon Hsiao-peng Lu, "Historical Introduction," *Transnational Chinese Cinemas: Identity, Nationhood, Gender*, ed. Sheldon Hsiao-peng Lu (Honolulu: University of Hawaii Press, 1997), pp. 1–31.

5   See Edward W. Said, *Orientalism* (New York: Vintage Books, 1979). Said examines the discourse of "Orientalism," i.e. the western literary colonization of the east for its own hegemonic advantage — and the "dynamic exchange between individual authors and the large political concerns shaped by the three great empires — British, French, American — in whose intellectual and imaginative territory the writing was

produced" (14–15). On a positive note, Said concludes: "I do believe ... that enough is being done today in the human sciences to provide the contemporary scholar with insights, methods, and ideas that could dispense with racial, ideological, and imperialist stereotypes of the sort provided during its historical ascendancy by Orientalism" (328). We will try in our enterprise to aspire to Said's intellectual challenge.

6   Rey Chow, "Film and Cultural Identity," in *The Oxford Guide to Film Studies*, ed. John Hill and Pamela Church Gibson (Oxford: Oxford University Press, 1998), p. 174.

7   Mike Featherstone, *Undoing Culture: Globalization, Postmodernism and Identity* (London: Sage Publications, 1995), p. 102.

8   Kwai-cheung Lo, *Chinese Face/Off: The Transnational Popular Culture of Hong Kong* (Urbana: University of Illinois Press, 2005), p. 111.

9   Walter Benjamin, "The Work of Art in the Age of Mechanical Reproduction," in *Illuminations: Walter Benjamin Essays and Reflections*, ed. Hannah Arendt (New York: Schocken Books, 1969), p. 234.

10   The Four Great Heavenly Kings (or Sky Kings) are Jacky Cheung, Leon Lai, Andy Lau, and Aaron Kwok, although they follow in the footsteps of singers like Sam Hui, Alan Tam, Kenny Bee, George Lam, Roman Tam, Danny Chan, and, of course, Leslie Cheung. The style emerged in the 1970s, with Cantonese-language-based lyrics written by the likes of Joseph Koo, in songs about everyday life set to western melodies and instrumentation. In the film the Kings are glimpsed in the front row of the appropriated footage of the music awards show.

11   The conflict between Rose and Leon Lai fans at the film's beginning mimics the war that raged between Leslie Cheung and Cantopop star Alan Tam Wing-lun fans in the mid-1980s, providing another in-joke. Cheung himself attributes this feud as part of the reason for his leaving Hong Kong for Vancouver (after taking Canadian citizenship, Cheung remained there for a year before returning to Hong Kong) because "I had much pressure. They liked to compare me to Ah Lun, which I hated." Cheung in June Lam's interview "Leslie Cheung's '98 Declaration: An Interview before the Golden Horse Awards," in *City Entertainment* 491 (5–13 February 1998): 16. Peter Chan would later use Leon Lai well in *Comrades* (1996), highlighting his vulnerability

and sweetness, but here he is the butt of several jokes. Known for his personal support of his largely female fan base and with a fan club of 5,000 (he's been dubbed "the Heavenly King of Fan Support"), the Beijing-born Lai is also derogatorily referred to as "Neon Leon," regarding his singing. See Jeff Yang, et al., *Eastern Standard Time: A Guide to Asian Influence on American Culture* (Boston: Mariner Books, 1997), p. 256. Of Lai's singing, "Love Hong Kong Film" reports, "People who can judge music better than I tell me his voice is nothing special." "Love Hong Kong Film," 20 May 2004, http://www.brns. com/hkactors/pages/page23.html.

12 Ackbar Abbas, in writing about *Crouching Tiger, Hidden Dragon*, and *In the Mood for Love*, discusses Hong Kong as emblematic of the "generic city," as identified by Peter Hall in *Cities in Civilization* and architect Rem Koolhas in "The Generic City," in *S, M, L, XL*, ed. Jennifer Sigler. Global cities are currently redesigning images for themselves, divorced from any history or identity, making them "generic" and invisible. See Ackbar Abbas, "Cinema, the City, and the Cinematic," in *Global Cities: Cinema, Architecture, and Urbanism in a Digital Age*, ed. Linda Krause and Patrice Petro (New Brunswick, New Jersey: Rutgers University Press, 2003), pp. 142–156.

13 Akbar Abbas, *Hong Kong: Culture and the Politics of Disappearance* (Minneapolis: University of Minnesota Press, 1997), p. 69.

14 Ibid., p. 81. In 1997 alone, there were ten reclamation projects ongoing, the most famous of which, the Chep Lak Kok Airport, opened in June 1998 with a new town of 200,000 near the airport adjacent to Lantau Island. In mid-2005, Hong Kong's population was 6.94 million, and its land growth through reclamation is now 1104 square kilometers (685.99 square miles). "About Hong Kong," 12 May 2007, http://www. info.gov.hk/info/hkbrief/eng/eng/ahk.htm.

15 Abbas, *Hong Kong*, p. 1.

16 David R. Meyer, "Hong Kong: Global Capital Exchange," in *Global Networks Linked Cities*, ed. Saskia Sassen (New York: Routledge, 2002), pp. 249–71.

17 See Peter Dicken, *Global Shift: Reshaping the Global Economic Map of the Twentieth Century*, 4th ed. (New York: Guilford Press, 2003). See also Michael Hoover and Lisa Odham Stokes, "Hong Kong in New York:

Global Connections, National Identity, and Filmic Representations," *New Political Science* 25.4 (December 2003): 509–32.

18   Meyer, p. 262.

19   Roland Robertson, "Comments on the Global Trend and Glocalization," in *Globalization and Indigenous Cultures*, ed. Nubutaka Inoue (Tokyo: Institute for Japanese Culture and Classics, 1997), pp. 217–25. Robertson, among others, has popularized the term. He traces it to articles in the late-1980s *Harvard Business Review*, penned by Japanese economists.

20   Steve Tsang, *A Modern History of Hong Kong* (Hong Kong: Hong Kong University Press, 2006), p. 269.

21   Ibid., p. 247.

22   Ibid., p. 248.

23   Rozanna Lilley, *Staging Hong Kong: Gender and Performance in Transition* (Honolulu: University of Hawai'i Press, 1998), p. 30.

24   Ibid., pp. 48–49.

25   Lo, p. 20.

26   Ibid., p. 118. One viewer's response included: "The scene in which Wing rattles off information about Sam and Rose reflects the absurdity of idolizing celebrities; digging through trash as if sifting through treasure."

27   An American South Korean female viewer in her 30s notes, "Interestingly, thinking about the film a day or so after watching it, I remembered the names of Sam and Rose, but I couldn't recall Wing's name too easily. Why was that? Was it by design? For foreign viewers, Sam and Rose are obviously easier to remember because they have American names (they've crossed-over? Claimed a western identity of sorts?), whereas Wing remains Chinese. But also, Sam and Rose remained pretty constant in their onscreen identities. So, maybe it was the play of identities (shifting, appropriating, boundary-crossing) that made Wing's name less memorable in the mind. I was asking myself what her name was — a boy's name? a girl's name? It finally did come to me, but it took awhile. At any rate, she wasn't etched into my memory as solidly as the other two, and I wonder if it was because her identity was unclear (by the director's design, or maybe just in my own subconscious). I watched it with a friend, and she

also seemed to remember Sam and Rose, but completely blanked on Wing's name." This spectator, bilingual in Korean and English, addresses Wing's superficial shifting identities in the story, but that she emphasizes the English names and "western identity" underscores Chan's global reach.

28   Although Tam is best known for Cantopop ballads, his early releases were sung more traditionally in a style derived from Cantonese opera, and he was known for precise articulation in a rich tenor. He often performed Cantonese opera, and the martial arts theme songs he sang mostly for television are more traditional in style. He continues to appeal to and remain popular with an older generation audience, despite his death in 2002.

29   The Beatles' release itself was a cover of an Isley Brothers' tune.

30   Interestingly, while directing the DreamWorks production *The Love Letter* (1999), Chan told Betsy Sherman that, although he had expected a big difference and was prepared for the worst, working on a Hollywood movie was "exactly the same" as shooting a Hong Kong movie, except for a bigger budget. The multi-lingual Chan confessed he sometimes forgot he was speaking English on the shoot. To this interviewer, he compared *The Love Letter* to a combination of *He's a Woman, She's a Man* and *Comrades* (1996) and noted differences between pre- and post-production in the two industries, citing the politics and bureaucracy for the difficulties of the former ("the process is so much more tiring because there's so much more bullshit and you have to deal with all these people") and its mixed bag results ("you have so much more time, you can try different versions ... [but] you also have all these people come in and suggest different versions, which is a drag, so you've got to deal with that again").

31   Gina Marchetti, *From Tian'anmen to Times Square: Transnational China and the Chinese Diaspora on Global Screens, 1989–1997* (Philadelphia: Temple University Press, 2006), pp. 31, 61–62.

32   Ibid.

33   In fact, in the sequel, Sam wears a Woody Allen mask at the opening costume party, just as both Anitas (Yuen and Mui) wear Whoopi Goldberg masks. The sequel also includes a riff on David O. Selznick's *Gone with the Wind* (1939) (ironically, Cheung also admired the film,

and took his English name, Leslie, from British actor Leslie Howard, whose role in the Civil War epic as Ashley Wilkes Cheung liked). Chan cites Stanley Donen's *Two for the Road* (1966) as a source that he had in mind for the sequel and Orson Welles's use of "rosebud" in *Citizen Kane* (1941) when he introduced the little rabbit as symbolic of Mui's character's search for her lost innocence. Yuen also fashions a mean Tina Turner when she attempts to sexualize herself to please Cheung's character in one scene in the sequel. With a film within the film in the sequel, Truffaut's *Day for Night* (1973) comes to mind, as well as *Jules and Jim* (1962) because of the love triangle between the three leads.

34 For many Western viewers, the film is reminiscent of Blake Edwards's *Victor/Victoria* (1982) but only superficially. Julie Andrews plays a singer who is a woman pretending to be a man pretending to be a woman. Robert Preston is a gay man (and her confidant), and James Gardner appears as the straight man that falls for the supposed female impersonator.

35 Director/producer Sydney Pollack describes *Tootsie* as a "story of a man masquerading as a woman who learns to be a better man." This description in some respects echoes the learning curve of Sam's character (but shifting the cross-dressing onto Wing). Furthermore, actor Dustin Hoffman, who played "Tootsie" in the movie, reflecting on that experience, explains that in life, he has learned "there were too many interesting women I never got to know because I was brainwashed. That movie was not a comedy for me." Hoffman alludes to sexist attitudes and condoned images of masculinity here, but by understanding *Tootsie* as drama, he comes close to Chan's conception of dramedy. Both interviewed in "AFI's [American Film Institute] 100 Years 100 Movies, Tenth Anniversary Edition," broadcast on CBS Television, 20 June 2007. *Tootsie* ranked #69.

36 Lo, pp. 108–11.

37 Ibid., p. 118.

38 Ng Ho, "A Preliminary Plot Analysis of Cantonese Comedy," in The 9th Hong Kong International Film Festival, *The Traditions of Hong Kong Comedy* (Hong Kong: Urban Council, 1985), p. 21.

39 Ibid., p. 22.

40   Cheng Yu, "The World According to Everyman," in The 9th Hong Kong International Film Festival, *The Traditions of Hong Kong Comedy* (Hong Kong: Urban Council, 1985), p. 41.

41   Ng, p. 24.

42   Anita Yuen's cute factor, innocence, and mugging in the film are reminiscent, for me at least, of the Japanese pop cultural product Hello Kitty, and there are numerous contemporary studies on this phenomenon. See, for example, Brian J. McVeigh, "How Hello Kitty Commodifies the Cute, Cool and Camp: 'Consumutopia' versus 'Control' in Japan." *Journal of Material Culture* 5.2 (2000): 225–45.

43   That Wing would win a male singing contest when 1) she is female, and 2) she cannot sing seems to be a matter of chance, and is explained in the film by the conflict between Sam and Rose. French theorist Roland Barthes would query, "But what is chance?" which applies here, in terms of the film action, but also in relation to life beyond the screen. That Wing's dreams come true echoes for Leslie Cheung's musical career; his first release, *Day Dreamin'* (1977), consisted entirely of his covering of American pop songs (including the likes of "Day Dreamer," "I Like Dreamin'," and "You Made Me Believe in Magic"). Sometimes dreams really do come true ...

44   Marchetti, p. 62.

45   Ironically, the handsome actor suffered permanent facial damage after a serious car accident in Danville, Kentucky while filming Edward Dmytryk's civil war epic *Raintree County* (1956). One side of his face was paralyzed and the actor required extensive reconstructive surgery. Elizabeth Taylor, Clift's co-star and friend, reportedly saved his life by removing two of his teeth that had lodged in his throat.

46   Benjamin, p. 231.

47   Quoted in Louis Giannetti, *Understanding Movies*, 10th ed. (Upper Saddle River, N.J.: Pearson/Prentice Hall, 2005), p. 300.

48   See Chapter 3 for use of the term "crossover" in another way. Cheung himself would release a collaborative album entitled *Crossover* (2002) with singer-songwriter Anthony Wong Yiu-ming (not to be confused with award-winning actor Anthony Wong Chau-sang, who also has several album releases). The Anthony Wong of *Crossover* is similar in his musical performance to Cheung, and known for his flamboyancy.

49 "Love HK Film," 20 May 2004, http://www.brns.com/hkactors/pages/
     page23.html.

50 Ibid.

51 Ibid.

52 Chan told film reviewer Betsy Sherman that he had "no problem" with
     first-time actors, that in fact, Anita Yuen and Leon Lai both got their
     starts with him. We should note that Teddy Chen's *Twenty-Something*,
     scripted by one of Peter Chan's partners at UFO, James Yuen, and
     produced by Peter Chan, was Jordan Chan's acting debut after his
     being discovered as a music television and concert dancer. *He's a
     Woman* was Jordan Chan's second film, released three months after
     Twenty-Something.

53 "Love Hong Kong Film."

54 Lisa Odham Stokes, "Spending Time with Yu: A Special Interview with
     Ronny Yu," *Asian Cult Cinema* 41: 58.

55 Pang Chai-choi and Lin Li, "Portraits of Ten Comedians," in The 9th
     Hong Kong International Film Festival, *The Traditions of Hong Kong
     Comedy* (Hong Kong: Urban Council, 1985), p. 62.

56 Cheung said, "John Woo a vraiment un cœur, pour tout, même s'il ne
     le montre pas sur un plateau. John Travolta, Nicolas Cage, l'ont dit.
     Dès que vous avez travaillé avec lui, vous vous ferier tuer pour lui ... *A
     Better Tomorrow* est un des films les plus important de ma carrière.
     Il a été le premier à m'expliquer plein de choses pour mon métier: où
     est la caméra, où est la lumière, comment avoir un meilleur angle sur
     l'écran ... Pendant les répétitions vous devez savoir exactement quel
     est l'angle de prises de vues, de la lumière. Cela m'a beaucoup aidé
     plus tard." Cheung's interview was translated into French from English,
     and published by Michel Ciment and Hubert Niogret as "Entretien
     Leslie Cheung: Dix-huit ans de travail acharne," in *Positif* 455 (January
     1999): 96–99.

57 Betsy Sherman, unpublished taped interview with Leslie Cheung; her
     article based on the interview appeared as "Hong Kong Star Cultivates
     US Audience," *Boston Globe*, 18 June 1997: D1+.

58 Ibid.

59 Yu quoted in Stokes, pp. 58–59. Of his work with Yu on *The Bride with
     White Hair*, Cheung remarked, "C'est une histoire très intéressante,

très romantique, d'amour et de trahison, traduite de manière très visuelle. C'est très dramatique." Ciment and Niogret, p. 99.

60 Lam, p. 16.

61 For an analysis of the Cheung-Wong collaborations, focusing on Leslie Cheung's characterizations as providing a thematic unity for Wong's narratives, see Gary Bettinson, "Reflections on a Screen Narcissist: Leslie Cheung's Star Persona in the Films of Wong Kar-wai," *Asian Cinema* 16: 1 (Spring/Summer 2005): 220–38.

62 In character as Sam, Cheung's lines include: "It's like this. Every business has its own rules. Just because I don't mind doesn't mean other people won't mind. Don't misunderstand me. I don't discriminate on this issue ... But I want to tell you that in the entertainment business, this is a very odd and sensitive issue. If you are [gay], just don't let anyone see it."

63 Siu-leung Li, *Cross-Dressing in Chinese Opera* (Hong Kong: Hong Kong University Press, 2003), p. 34.

64 Ibid.

65 Lam, p. 13.

66 Purported a love song about a couple's conflict, the song lyrics include lines like "It's like in parades and performances,/ your eyesight can only touch one side of my face/ Being obsessed with the flashing expressions/ You actually know only one side of my face/ Do you know me clearly?/ Do you understand me?" It is tempting to relate them to Cheung's personal conflicts, regarding assimilating his image with the real Cheung Kwok-wing. It strikes me as so very sad that someone with so much exuberance and life when he was "on," was evidently in so much pain, and that the obvious signs and proclamations were so blatant they were unseen.

67 Abbas introduces Holbein's image in relation to Hong Kong architecture, specifically the non-descript ski-slope modernist style Hong Kong Cultural Center, which preserved the Hong Kong–Canton Railway clock tower on its site. Abbas claims the tower is too easily seen, therefore brings about the disappearance of history and keeps the viewing subject in its place. I think the technique and Holbein's image in particular fit Cheung's masking/unmasking and Chan's use of the local. See Abbas, *Hong Kong*.

68 Conflating gay politics and the celebrity factors of *He's a Woman*, in real life, Cheung and his longtime partner, "Daffy" Tong, were outed by paparazzi. During Cheung's funeral, Tong appeared as and was treated like the grieving widow, and he was obviously in enormous pain.

69 Preceding the encore, stylishly dressed in a tuxedo, following his appearing in numerous glittery and form-fitting sequined costumes, as well as the sparkling red high heels (shades of Dorothy in *The Wizard of Oz*), Cheung very intimately and straightforwardly delivered the following: "First of all, I want to thank you, my audience here at the Hong Kong Coliseum. It's thanks to everyone I was brought back to this stage tonight. To be here on this very stage, I am a very, very lucky person, because of your support. Okay. Tonight is an exceptional evening as it is New Year's. [Cheers from the audience.] Okay. Before my encore, I would like to say a few words. Why? Because I haven't been a grateful son. It has been over ten years from the time I started singing. I have performed many concerts. My mother has attended each one to share in my happiness. There hasn't been one time when I have actually sung a song for her. My mummy is here tonight [acknowledges her in audience]. Mummy, how did you give birth to such a cute and gorgeous son? [Cheung smiling, cheers from audience]. Is it because you were extremely happy with Daddy? Extremely high? [Laughter] Mummy, tonight I dedicate this song to you and to another person who is very close to my heart, your godchild. At my lowest point he gave me several months' salary to help me through the rough times. He is my great friend Mr. Tong. Now I would like to dedicate this song to my dearest friend and family. The song I am about to share with everyone here tonight is by Teresa Teng." ["The Moon Represents My Heart" follows]. "Thank you. New Year's is here. First of all, Happy New Year, everyone. I wish you peace and happiness, longevity, and friendship forever." [Then Cheung sings "Chase."]

70 Mo appeared, while pregnant, in Cheung's directorial debut, *From Ashes to Ashes* (2000).

71 Many Chinese people, in Hong Kong and the diaspora, have commented, with superstition, on Cheung's final film, *Inner Senses/ Yee diy hung gaan/Yidu kongjian* (2002), in which the actor played a psychiatrist trying to help a patient haunted by ghosts when he

himself is haunted by a ghost that, through adolescent guilt, almost convinces him to jump from a building. Cheung was reportedly afraid of heights, and many believe there were bad spirits on the set of the film, leading to Cheung's suicide.

72 June Lam, "Leslie Cheung: Behind the Legend," *City Entertainment* 520 (18 March–1 April 1999): 26–30. The translator of this article noted how much of the language included current Hong Kong slang, reflecting the hipness and quickness with which such vernacular changes, similar to Hong Kong as a global site itself.

73 Cheung also told Lam, "Last year [1998] was not a good year for me. This year [1999] so far is going well." Ibid.

74 Lisa Odham Stokes, "Cheung, Leslie Kwok-wing," in *Historical Dictionary of Hong Kong Cinema* (Lanham, MD: Scarecrow Press, 2007), pp. 76–79.

75 Ingrained anti-homosexual beliefs in Hong Kong can be seen in the discussion that took place during the Hong Kong Legislative Council's meeting regarding the Crimes (Amendment) Bill that when passed effectively decriminalized homosexuality. On the one hand, there were adamant homophobes; as in the rhetorical bombast below:

Mr. David Cheung Chi-kong, JP: "Homosexuality is a kind of deviant behavior which cannot be condoned socially. People try to rationalize the act by saying that it is a matter of sexual preference. It is not. Such deviant behavior, whatever its cause behind it, needs to be cured ... Homosexuality has often been defended as a matter of human rights. It is sheer nonsense. Who does not respect basic human rights but how can one condone wrong doings in the name of human rights?"

Mr. Kingsley Sit Ho-yin: "I ... notice that there are many students up in the public gallery. Their purpose in coming here is probably not to learn about the decriminalization of homosexuality but to see how the Legislative Council works. But what the Legislative Council is discussing today is the decriminalization or, in other words, the legalization, of homosexuality. I believe that this will have a huge impact on young people. If it is said that it is not illegal for two male persons to engage in homosexual acts in private, then they will perhaps ask, 'Does this mean that it is legal?' I hope that my young friends in the public gallery will ignore what some Members say and will not, for the sake of human rights, take the path leading to homosexuality ... . I want to ask Members, if you go home tonight after this meeting and receive a sudden phone call telling you that your son or daughter is homosexual or lesbian, how would you feel, sad or happy?"

Mr. Pang Chun-hoi, MBE: "Today the Crimes (Amendment) Bill 1991 was passed. Is this reasonable? Homosexuality (buggery) is against the Chinese tradition, which is considered evil by Chinese. Now it is a rape of public opinion to allege decriminalization represents the majority view of the people. Is this really what the public wants?"

On the other hand, there were those more liberal and enlightened views that still reflected ingrained prejudices. These speakers were defensive about condoning homosexuality, some explaining they did not approve of the practice, but at least recognizing the reality of the presence of homosexuals in society and the human rights issue involved:

Dr. Leong Che-hung: "Let me from the outset, Sir, stress that I do not condone homosexuality nor do I favor that homosexuality should be glorified. Instead, I would like to extend the views of the medical profession on homosexuality which might perhaps shed light on its decriminalization."

Mr. Martin Lee Chu-ming, QC, JP: "I came in time to hear a rhetorical question posed to this Council by the Honorable David Cheung. He asked, 'Do we want our children to engage in homosexuality?' Well, the answer to that question is clearly no, but I am afraid it does not solve the problem because if our children should be born that way inclined then the question is: Do we want to see them punished with imprisonment or by the imposition of a fine? As for Mr. Kingsley Sit's other rhetorical question that if we are told that our own children in fact are engaged in homosexual acts will we be happy or will we be sad? The answer clearly, Sir, is that we will be sad but the question is: Supposing Mr. Kingsley Sit will be shocked with that news no doubt, he too will be sad, but does he want his children to be punished with imprisonment or fine?"

The secretary for security clarified (reassured?) the voting body by explaining:

Mr. Alistair Peter Asprey, OBE, AE, JP: "The Bill does not advocate or seek to encourage homosexuality. The provisions in the Bill prohibiting the public display of homosexual acts, the corruption of the young persons and homosexual acts committed other than in private will be strictly enforced."

See the record through the Hong Kong government's official website at http://www.legco.gov.hk /yr90-91/english/lc_sitg/hansard/ h910710.pdf.

On a more optimistic note, director Shu Kei, having directed *A Queer Story (Gay Man at 40/Gei lui 40/Ji lao 40*, 1997), a drama starring George Lam and Jordan Chan in a generation gap homosexual relationship, describes an experience with a positive future for young people and an ideal world (as contrasted to Sit above): "We held a preview of *A Queer Story* (on 31 December 1996) and I went to the theatre to see the response. Nearly 80% of the audience were people under 25. They had a very open attitude and were not burdened by morals. This made me very happy. I found out that my worries only apply to people of my own age group, and people from the same social class. Young people don't have our worries and burdens. I want to portray a world without worries. Sometimes it occurs to me that when young people waver between homosexuality and heterosexuality, they are going through a process of exploration, a process of choosing." Quoted in "*A Queer Story*: Shu Kei," interviewed by Linda Lai and Kim Choi, in *Hong Kong Panorama 96–97*, The Hong Kong International Film Festival (Hong Kong: Urban Council of Hong Kong, 1997) p. 35.

76   See Lilley, p. 216.

77   What amounted to stalking and harassment of gays was a regular practice by Hong Kong's Special Investigations Unit (SIU), and officers would enter gay bars demanding names, ages, professions, frequency of visits, and names of friends. Many feared this intelligence gathering would be provided to the Mainland Chinese with the 1997 return. See Lilley, p. 215. This situation is reminiscent of the gay witch hunts undergone by homosexuals and others in urban US areas such as New York, Chicago, and San Francisco in the 1950s and 1960s. In the US, such harassment eventually led to the Stonewall Riots of June 1969 in

New York City, with days of protests, demonstrations, and violence. (See Note 32 in Chapter 3.) Stonewall births the Gay Liberation movement, and Gay Pride marches began in June 1970 in New York City, San Francisco, Chicago, and Los Angeles, to commemorate the event. Stonewall stands symbolically as the voice for gay rights, and towards the end of June is globally commemorated with gay rights events celebrating the beginning of the movement. Even Walt Disney World in Orlando, Florida celebrates Gay Days, specifically targeting gay guests in June. Cultural and political differences have delayed Hong Kong's reaction to oppression, and the China specter remains, but at the same time Hong Kong's current gay movement replicates what has occurred elsewhere, with gay pride out of the closet and voiced.

78   The Basic Law, mandated by the Joint Declaration, consists of 9 Chapters with 160 Articles and 3 Annexes. Chapter III, Fundamental Rights and Duties of Residents, consists of 19 Articles, none of which address the rights of sexual minorities. Article 37 states, "The freedom of marriage of Hong Kong residents and their right to raise a family freely shall be protected by law." Article 38 states, "Hong Kong residents shall enjoy the rights and freedoms safeguarded by the laws of the Hong Kong Special Administrative Region." Regarding the rights of sexual minorities, many perceived that the articles were too generalized overall, and the 37th article here certainly reifies heterosexual norms. See http://www.info.gov.hk/basic_law/facts/index.htm.

79   Travis S. K. Kong, "Queering Masculinity in Hong Kong Movies," in *Masculinities and Hong Kong Cinema*, ed. Lai-kwan Pang and Day Wong (Hong Kong: Hong Kong University Press, 2005), pp. 58–80.

80   See Fredric Jameson, *Postmodernism or, The Cultural Logic of Late Capitalism* (Durham, N.C.: Duke University Press, 1991).

81   *The Warlords* was released on 1000 screens across China, the widest ever release at that time, and it became the sixth biggest earner (over US$ 12 million) of 2007 in just four days. See Patrick Frater, "'Warlords' Slays Box Office in China: Chan's Action Movie Nets $12.2 Million," *Variety*, 17 December 2007. 12 June 2008. http://www.variety.com/article/VR1117977856.html.

82   From http://www.sina.com.

Chapter 5   Audience

1   "Lost in America" [Interview by Gavin Smith], *Film Comment* 42.4 (July/August 2006): 28.

2   Personal Interview, Ronny Yu, 17 October 1998.

3   "Lost in America."

4   Tsui quoted in Craig D. Reid, "Interview with Tsui Hark," *Film Quarterly* 48 (Spring 1995): 39.

5   Holland, in *The Dynamics of Literary Response* (London: Oxford University Press, 1968), suggested that creative works are comprised of fantasies that usually would lead to anxiety, but by the "artist" evoking form and meaning, satisfactory experiences result. Holland perceived form and meaning as defense mechanisms that transformed unconscious fantasies into acceptable ideas (subconscious versus conscious). As he continued developing his theory, as in *Poems in Persons* (New York: Norton, 1973; rev. 2000) and *5 Readers Reading* (New Haven: Yale, 1975), Holland suggested we could read the author's and the readers' personality in core identity themes; readers' personalities control their readings. Holland says we all have core themes, as authors (filmmakers) and readers (viewers) that we let play, endlessly varied, in our lives, and when we work/write, we do so in the same style, but change our content as we change.

6   Norman Holland, *Journal of the Society of Cinematologists* 3 (1963): 18. Rebecca Bell-Metereau cites this passage from Holland in *Hollywood Androgyny*, 2nd ed. (New York: Columbia University Press, 1993), p. 17.

7   See Miriam Hansen, "Early Silent Cinema: Whose Public Sphere?", *New German Critique* 29 (Spring–Summer 1983): 147–84. The study alluded to is German sociologist Altenloh's doctoral dissertation entitled *Zur Soziologie des Kino* (1914).

8   See Metz, *Film Language: A Semiotics of the Cinema* (Chicago: University of Chicago Press, 1974).

9   Imagine contemporary audience reception as contrasted with today's audience in a film like LeRoy Prinz's campy musical comedy *All-American Co-ed* (1941). The movie was advertised as "the season's gayest musical," and starred Johnny Downs as Bob Sheppard/Bobbie

De Wolfe. The thinly disguised plot features the Quinceton follies, in
which all the frat brothers perform in drag, but the joke gets taken to
an extreme when the boys decide Bob will impersonate a Mar Brynn
co-ed to gain entry to the all-girls' school. As "Queen of the Flowers,"
Bobbie falls for a fellow student, and it's only a matter of time (53
minutes, the film's length) before the ruse is discovered and resolved.
"Looks like love has crossed us up," he tells the lucky girl. The movie
is full of double entendres. "You do have a lot of boyfriends," the girl
tells Bobbie, who adds, "just brothers." The female Mar Brynn
president says, "There will be no men on campus as long as I'm
president," to which her mousy male assistant replies, "I'm a man."
"You're safe," she answers. Like *He's a Woman*, this story concludes
with the happiness of the heterosexual couple.

10   Bell-Metereau, p. xiv.

11   Benjamin, p. 234.

12   Derrida spoke at the University of Florida when I was a graduate
student in the late 1970s–early 1980s. Professor John Levy in the
English Department was his current translator at the time. This remark
has stuck with me for many years, and I continue to believe it speaks
volumes, considering the current world crisis.

13   Benjamin, p. 234.

14   I am adapting Wolfgang Iser's concept of "reading as a selfish act."
See *The Act of Reading: A Theory of Aesthetic Response* (Baltimore:
Johns Hopkins University Press, 1978). Referents as far afield as
Chance the Gardener's "I like to watch" in Hal Ashby's *Being There*
(1969), a wonderful filmic representation of Jerzy Kozinski's novel of
the same title (adapted to the screen by the author) and Roland Barthes
and Jacques Derrida also come to mind ("the pleasure of the text,"
"there is nothing outside the text") in thinking about the immense
pleasure of involving yourself in a movie.

15   Ben Wasserstein, "The Man With 50,000 Friends: How Kevin Smith
Accidentally Invented the Future of Movie Marketing," *New York*, 24
July 2006: 64.

16   James Harvey, *Romantic Comedy in Hollywood: From Lubitsch to
Sturges* (New York: Knopf, 1987), p. 672.

17 June Lam, "Leslie Cheung's '98 Declaration: An Interview before the Golden Horse Awards," *City Entertainment* 491 (5–13 February 1998): 16.

18 Wilder was extensively informally interviewed in an office space by German director Volker Schlöndorff (*The Tin Drum*), but Wilder was concerned about the bare bones filmmaking style used, and asked that none of the footage be made public until his death. Schlöndorff honored the request, and with Gisela Grischow, finally released the documentary *Billy Wilder Speaks*, Bioskop Film, 2006.

19 Stanley Fish, "Interpreting the Variorum," *Critical Inquiry* 2.3 (Spring 1976): 465–85.

20 Ibid., p. 474.

21 Ibid., p. 485.

22 The credits opening the film feature Leslie Cheung first, with Anita Yuen and Carina Lau listed on the same line below him. Considering the gender politics inside and outside the film, this provides another way of thinking about men on top.

23 "Love and Bullets Hong Kong DVD Reviews," 30 September 2005, http://www.loveandbullets.com/hesawoman.htm.

24 "A Better Tomorrow Hong Kong Movies Coming Soon to DVD," 30 September 2005, http://www.abtdvd.com/reviews/hesawomanshesaman.htm.

25 "Hong Kong Movie Database," 30 September 2005, http://www.hkmdb.com/db/movies/reviews.mhtml?id=7871&displayset=eng.

26 See Benjamin R. Barber, *Jihad vs. McWorld* (New York: Times Books, 1995).

27 Erik Erikson, *Childhood and Society* (New York: Norton, 1950 [1993]), pp. 261–62.

28 See Metz, *Film Language: A Semiotics of the Cinema* (Chicago: University of Chicago Press, 1974).

29 See Quintin Hoare and Geoffrey Nowell Smith, *Selections from the Prison Notebooks of Antonio Gramsci* (New York: International Publishers, 1980) and Michel Foucault, *Power/Knowledge: Selected Interviews and Other Writings 1972–1977*, ed. Colin Gordon (New York: Pantheon, 1980).

30   Cheng Yu, "The World According to Everyman," in The 9th Hong Kong International Film Festival, *The Traditions of Hong Kong Comedy* (Hong Kong: Urban Council, 1985), p. 41.

31   Ibid., p. 42.

32   Figures provided by *Hong Kong Film 1994–1995*, a publication of the Hong Kong, Kowloon and New Territories Motion Picture Industry Association, Ltd.

33   Making the sequel was part of the deal Chan had made with Golden Harvest to save UFO, after the failure (critically and at the box office) of his heartfelt *The Age of Miracles* (*Ma ma fan fan*, 1996), the film that followed *He's a Woman*. Golden Harvest took over UFO (eventually selling its library to Warner Brothers), but added to the package was Chan's request that he could also make a small film, which became the sleeper success *Comrades, Almost a Love Story* (*Honeysweet*) (*Tim mat mat/Tian mi mi*, 1996).

34   An American South Korean 30-something female explains, "Although the sequel is sort of an inversion of the first movie, and the gender relations get doubly complex, it's still the female impersonating the male. Fish's [Yu Lo] dressing up as a woman to get the lesbian girl seemed to be thrown in there to balance this out somehow."

35   A recent US comedy *Blades of Glory* (2007), starring Will Ferrell and Jon Heder and directed by Will Speck and Josh Gordon, set in the world of competitive figure skating, provides ample opportunity for comparison and contrast to Chan's two films. In some respect dealing with a similar theme, what I will term "gay anxiety," both challenge the straight/gay binary opposition, and both are set in their respective entertainment worlds, with an insider's look at what goes into making the images for the fans. But *Blades* remains a comedy, not a dramedy, and its physical humor and crotch jokes overwhelm — the gangly Ferrell in a full body stocking and the blonde Prince Charming hairstyle of Hedder pretty much says it all; it lacks Chan's light touch and dramedy style. Owen Gleiberman's take on the Hollywood movie is spot on: "*Blades of Glory* is a farce of preening emasculation in spandex. It is also, undeniably, a mild comedy of homosexual panic, though in a place as sexually clenched as America, no one, from either the left or the right, has much to fear from a good, honest gay-anxiety

joke. Remember the one that popped up in the middle of the Super Bowl — that commercial, with two men nibbling away at different ends of a candy bar, only to end up in a kiss? It tickled you in two directions at once, turning homophobia into a sly *what if?* There are moments in *Blades of Glory* with a similar effect." Gleiberman's observation about an uptight US is similar to our noting the ingrained anti-homosexual attitudes prevalent in Hong Kong. Further proving the uptightness of societies in reference to sexual orientation, the commercial to which the film reviewer refers was pulled shortly after the Super Bowl, considered too controversial. Owen Gleiberman, "Icemen Cometh," *Entertainment Weekly*, 6 April 2007: 55.

36 Michael Parenti, *Inventing Reality: The Politics of News Media* (New York: St. Martin's Press, 1993). Although Parenti's study focuses on the news media, his approach is useful when applied to entertainment, both on television and onscreen.

37 Figures provided by Ms. Roberta Chin of Golden Harvest via email 17 October 2005.

38 Caroline Evans and Lorraine Gamman, in "Reviewing Queer Viewing" criticize Mulvey's analysis for ignoring spectatorial fluidity, and they turn to Roland Barthes early work on cultural coding to make room for polymorphous identifications and queer viewing (regardless of the sexual orientation of the spectator). See "Reviewing Queer Viewing," in *Queer Cinema, The Film Reader*, ed. Harry Bennoff and Sean Griffin (New York: Routledge, 2004), pp. 209–24.

39 See psychoanalyst Lionel Ovesey on pseudohomosexuality, a behavior whereby heterosexuals exhibit anxieties over their sexual identities and if displaying homosexual behavior are reluctant to be labeled as homosexual. Lionel Ovesey, *Homosexuality and Pseudohomosexuality* (New York: Science House, 1969).

40 Nip Miu-fong and Mimi Lam, "Twenty Years of Cantonese Comedy: Five Interviews," in The 9th Hong Kong International Film Festival, *The Traditions of Hong Kong Comedy* (Hong Kong: Urban Council, 1985), p. 76.

41 Mast, p. 17.

Credits

He's a Woman, She's a Man (Golden Branch, Jade Leaf)/Gam chi yuk yip **(1994)**

Director
Peter Ho-sun Chan

Producer
Peter Ho-sun Chan

Screenplay
James Yuen Sai-sang
Lee Chi-ngai
Peter Ho-sun Chan

Cinematographer
Joe Chan Jun-git

Editor
Chan Kei-hop

Lighting
Siu Chi-ming

Production Designer
Hai Chung-man
Lau Man-wa

Music
Clarence Hui Yuen
Chui Tsang-hei
Lyrics Lam Chik

Costume Designer
Dora Ng Lei-lo

Executive Producer
Claudie Chung Chun

Production Company
United Filmmakers Organization (UFO)

Distributor
Mandarin Films

Cast
Leslie Cheung Kwok-wing (Sam Koo)
Anita Yuen Wing-yee (Lam Ji-wing)
Carina Lau Ka-ling (Rose)
Jordan Chan Siu-chun (Yu Lo, Fish)
Eric Tsang Chi-wai (Auntie)
Jerry Lam Hiu-fung (George)
Law Kar-ying (Joseph)
Cheung Suet-ling (Alice)

Lawrence Cheng Tan-shui (Mo Chow-chu)
Clarence Hui-yuen (Wing's vocal coach)
Nelson Cheung Hok-yun (party cameo)
Lee Hiu-tung (Fung Bobo)
Patrick Tsui Kwok-keung (Paul)
Joe Cheung Tung-cho (Peter)
Mantic Yiu Chi-wan (Peter's wife)
Jacob Cheung Chi-leung (MTV director)
Lee Ho-lam (Roger)
Ng Chin-yan (Chesty Lin)
Chan Wai-lung (Wing's dance coach)

Filmography

Peter Ho-sun Chan

2002 *Three/Saam gang* omnibus with two other directors, Kim Hee-woon (*Memories*) and Nonzee Nimibutr (*The Wheel*); Chan's contribution (*Going Home*)

2002 *Golden Chicken/Gam gai* (co-producer)

2004 *Golden Chicken 2/Gam gai 2* (co-producer)

2004 *The Eye 2/Gin gwai 2* (co-producer)

2005 *Three ... Extremes/Saam gang* (co-producer)

2005 *The Eye 10 (The Eye 3)/Gin gwai 10* (co-producer)

2005 *Perhaps Love/Ruoguo ai*

2006 *McDull, the Alumni* (co-producer)

2007 *Protégé/Munto* (producer)

2007 *The Warlords/Tau ming chong*